*Nehru Bal Pustakalaya*



# MIR SPACE STATION

## WE WILL RETURN AND PICK STARS

**Violet Razeghpanah**

*English Translation*
**Shirin Rahbari (Samii)**

*Illustrations*
**Harinder Singh**

एकः सूते सकलम्

**NATIONAL BOOK TRUST, INDIA**

Originally written in Persian language, this book has been awarded UNESCO First Prize of Children and Young Adults Literature for Peace and Tolerance for the year 2001.

ISBN 978-81-237-3980-9

First Edition 2002
Reprints 2004, 2008, 2012 (*Saka* 1934)



₹ 50.00

Published by the Director, National Book Trust, India
Nehru Bhawan, 5 Institutional Area, Phase-II
Vasant Kunj, New Delhi-110 070

# Introduction

Perhaps it is for the first time in our literature that science is the subject of a fictional story. However, despite it being scientific and imaginary, it can not be placed in the category of science fiction. In normal methods of writing science fiction, the author tries to be true to the limitations that nature dictates as scientific laws. However, science is more a means of expressing that which man is not able to achieve, at least for the moment; travelling to the planets of the solar system seems more accessible to the empire of the Milky Ways, which is beyond the imagination of mankind.

But science is the axis in this story. The author has been quite careful about points directly related to science that should completely comply with scientific realities and facts. Actually, at the beginning it seems that the main goal of the author is to deal with certain aspects of science and its derivatives in the form of a story; the movement of satellites, different reasons for dispatching them and the way of life of astronauts in space stations. However, the story in its entirety reveals that the author has also been concerned with other subjects, for example, tending to common concerns of man. It is appropriate here to point out certain outstanding characteristics of this work. First, this is among the few cases in which science is not portrayed in the form of highly advanced and destructive weapons and war machines which destroy and distract another planet from a great distance. (For the common man, usually, science is experienced by Einstein and his discovery of the atom bomb. They do not consider thousands of other scientific innovations that have served man). Here, the main role of science is to solve the problems of human beings in all aspects of life.

Another important point in this story is tending to problems beyond everyday and usual concerns. The pollution of the environment, destruction of forests, the extinction of various flora and fauna, the disappearance of the ozone layer and similar cases have been mentioned as dangers which face the whole of the planet earth and its inhabitants. Therefore, all the countries in the world are faced with these problems and we cannot pretend that it is the problem of 'powerful' countries and pass over it easily.

A global problem needs a global solution, and a global solution can only be achieved through friendship and understanding among nations. This point that has been portrayed by the camaraderie between five youngsters from five different corners of the earth, participating in the 'plan', is among the outstanding particulars of this story.

In principle, why is tending to science, and especially in literature, important? From one view, it can be said that discussing scientific concepts in the form of stories is very effective in learning. In this light, a story is solely a means for teaching particular concepts. An old method which is normally recommended and used; but paying attention to science in the domain of literature is important in another aspect. Today, science has made life complicated. Because of the direct effect of science and its derivatives in our lives, it is of utmost importance that it becomes common knowledge. For this very reason, in countries where science has found its place, more attention is paid to its expansion. In other words, as science grows and becomes more complete, its instruments become more sophisticated. Naturally, this complication demands a more sophisticated manner of thinking in life. For the expansion of science, and to allow society to keep abreast of its progress, the sophistication of thought must be made public. In other words, science must find its place among the people. The influence of science in a progressive society is the apparent method of scientific thinking, or better said, is that modern manner of thought is in all aspects of human culture, which itself enhances the development of science.

However, the establishment of a new thought does not happen on its own. Like the process of a scientific work, the endeavour to develop a scientific thought is a conscious effort which is up to and should be carried out by the learned and intellectual individuals in a society. Certainly, in a society where the process of development has progressed in a smooth and natural manner, all sectors of society grow, harmoniously influencing each other. Therefore, Jules Verne's 'Trip to the Moon' is as primitive as the train of his era. But it is not so for us. We import the products of developed cultures in separate pieces and thus we are not able to see the complications and unity hidden in them. This insight is not seen even in the limits of science itself or the scientific realms. This insight must be developed and this is possible only when the advanced sections of society progress side by side. Paying attention to the simple fact that the countries with style in art and literature are the same as those with advanced science, displays this relationship in those countries. This rapport is inherent in the infrastructure of these societies in an organized manner. Therefore, an author or an artist becomes familiar with this type of outlook from the first years of his or her life, and he or she himself or herself will in his or her turn enhance its expansion and growth. However, in this country, we have to learn by ourselves. This learning is not only to know how to write about science, it is necessary for understanding of the complication of our present world. In reality, literature and the art of our country can become international, so that they can bridge the gap between our local and global problems; and understanding the global problems can only be reached by a new way of thinking.

The first science fiction in our children's literature happens on the ship of peace and its message is peace and friendship. It is interesting to note that the place where the story unfolds is across all boundaries. This can be attributed to the optimism of the author, and her outlook on the future. An outlook which can be found only in the short period of the re-development and flourishment of Persian literature in the first centuries of Hejri* and after that, especially in recent years we have little sign of it. It is hoped that this aspect of literature, for the reasons pointed out will be more focused upon.

Dr MANSUR VESALI
Faculty of Physics
University of Shahid Rajaee
Editor-in-Chief of the Journal of Astrology

* *Encyclopedia for Young People*, Volume 2 (A), p. 148, Flourishment of Persian Literature (in Persian).

## Author's Introduction

Sometimes, certain things happen in life, like chasing beautiful butterflies, that take us far, far away and stir the flighty imagination. Just as what happened to me on hearing about the Mir Station. Immediately I asked myself what is Mir? What is it doing in space? What is its goal and how is it stationary in space? Then this became an objective and my mind became preoccupied with finding out about the space station that circled around the earth. I searched in several books, with the hope that maybe they would give me some information, but I didn't find much. I visited the Children's Book Council, I knew that Mrs. Touran Mirhadi and the intellectuals, researchers and artists who collaborate with her, were in the midst of authoring an encyclopedia for the children and young adults of our country. From there I returned with an armful of information. Dr. Vesali, whose views you read in the introduction, lent me two video films and an article in English, about the Mir Station. After that an article in Hamshahri newspaper attracted my attention. In the latter, an astronaut who had been stationed in Mir, had written his memoirs of that place for his newborn baby. However, all of this did not seem enough, there were still a number of points that were not clear to me.

Benefitting from the information in two encyclopedias, I learned about the flight of Mir and its structure. Finally, the internet lit the dark corners of knowledge in my mind. Thus, the time came to travel to the Mir Station, with children; children whose wishes and goals are very high, even higher than the atmosphere. Travel to the station that belongs to the Russians. But with the keys of science each lock is opened and every obstacle is pushed aside. This magic key not only took the children and us over the boundaries and Russia, but helped us converse with outstanding space scientists of that land who taught us a lot. Then we became travelers of Soyuz and thus we traveled to the Mir Station. In good time, everything was perfected. Our objective, our love for all mankind, for our Mother Earth, even our melody and our song. My song became more beautiful and whole, when with the help of Mr. Tabatabaii I was able to correlate it with the translation of the words of a foreign song called 'Stay Hope', the result of which is the song of friendship, unity and hope that children read at the end of the story.

I hear their voices and say: No sound is sweeter than the melody of peace, love, friendship and understanding. With the hope that at the end of the Mir Station you will have some belief.

Finally, I would like to express my gratitude to Mrs. Turan Mirhadi, for introducing my work to UNESCO, Mrs. Nooshin Ansari for kindly translating the summary of this book, Dr. Mansur Vesali, Mr. Kazem Tabatabaii, Mrs. Vida Lashgari and my publisher Mrs. Mahvash Kianvash, Hamshahri newspaper and all those who made this trip possible for us.

Spring 1999 VIOLET RAZEGH-PANAH

I would like to express my sincere thanks to Mrs. Shirin Rahbari (Samii) who has graciously translated this book into English, for the children of the world.

Summer 2001 Violet Razegh-Panah

# 1

Mr. Brosky was sitting in a comfortable armchair. The five of us were sitting around a round table and were listening to him. He had arranged this meeting to introduce us to each other and to inform us of the trip's plan. His blue eyes roamed on each of our faces. His white skin had gotten old and his double-chin moved when he talked. He said:

"We enter the world of knowledge when we are old and decrepit. Now we have everything except time. Time is precious. So much so that no one can pay the price. Therefore, we chose outstanding students and the ones who placed first in the science Olympiads. You are the masters of time; owners of time. Kids, the planet earth has become ill, try to save her. Make the best of this opportunity. Scientists are willing to help you in any way. Above all, we want this planet to be healthy for you and your peers..."

Last year, when it was announced that I was among the top students, Mr. Brosky wrote a letter and invited me.

After the Foreign Ministry of my country gave me permission to make this trip, I wrote them a letter and informed them that I could participate in this trip. Then I started reading and studying books and articles which were sent to me in English. The fact that I was actually going on this trip was a dream and a wish coming true. So I was studying hard, and by going to classes I improved my English... and today I am in Moscow, with four

other youths from other countries.

My eyes caught the sight of the large, glass globe which was placed on the book shelf, the mountains and the plains and the seas were all shown in different coloured glass. It was a large room, with tall narrow windows, through which the sunlight had penetrated the room diagonally. I was tired of sitting down and I wanted to go to the window and look outside, and I also wished to play with the glass globe, but Mr. Brosky was still talking. He said: 'It was my suggestion that we should teach and ask the opinion of the young people who had placed first in the science Olympiads, in connection with the reconstruction of our planet. It is not right that youngsters with so much capability and diligence should do the same things that other children do. We'll see what you can do. Here is the ball and the field, as they say. Now stand up one by one and introduce yourself... He turned his face to Nooshka and said: "Nooshka, I will start with you."

With his long blond hair, red face, a masculine figure and a little fat, Nooshka got up from his chair and with a smile said: "Nooshka, from Russia".

The kids lowered their heads and laughed discreetly. Fredrick mumbled: "Polar bear!" All of a sudden, we all burst out laughing. Mr. Brosky looked at us with surprise but tried not to show anything. Helmut, with his white face and wavy hair and eyes that were full of mischief stood up. He put his hands on the table and smilingly said: "I am Helmut from Germany!" Nooshka murmured: "An unworthy earth-worm!" We smirked again. Grippingly, Helmut said to Nooshka: "Excuse me bookworm!" Nooshka answered: "Yes, I had forgotten." Mr. Brosky was confused, and couldn't understand us. Like all teachers, he looked serious and said: "What is the laughter for?" Helmut smoothed his hair and said: "Sir, my nickname is "bookworm", but Nooshka, mistakenly, called me 'earthworm', I had to correct him." Mr. Brosky said: "How does he know your nickname?" Innocently, Helmut said: "They gave me this nickname last night." Mr. Brosky's eyes became as wide as possible. After a while he said hesitantly: "Why did you give Helmut such an ugly nickname?"

Matsu, who came from Japan, got up and said: "Because he gave us nicknames as well." Then, he brushed his straight and full hair from his forehead and started laughing. Mr. Brosky asked: "For example what did he call you?" All of us loudly said in one voice: "Bat."

Mr. Brosky laughed heartily and said: "But why?!" The kids pointed towards Matsu's eyes which were as small as two peas and said: "Because of his big eyes!" The sound of Mr. Brosky's laughter was very loud and the employees of the space center who had never heard his laughter came into the room with various excuses and looked at him with surprise. Mr. Brosky's glance fell on me and he gestured me to introduce myself. I said: "This is Abtin from Iran," when the kids yelled together: "Bespectacled snake!" Mr. Brosky had become excited and was clapping his hands and laughing. He said: "Why a snake? Do you bite?" I said: "No sir, from ancient times a snake has been known as a symbol of wisdom and knowledge." Matsu and Helmut started whis-

tling. The employees had gathered in the room, and as though we had put on a show, they were watching us. Mr. Brosky had pointed at Fredrick. He got up and carefully looked at everyone. He had dark skin and frizzy hair. His teeth were white and large, and when he laughed or talked would shine in his face. With a prolonged smile, he said: "This is Frederick from America." Helmut said: "He is only a black cow." The employees started an uproar. The sounds became louder. The sound of laughter and discussion filled the room. Mr. Brosky whose face had became flushed and whose eyes sparkled, said: "Oh, poor Frederick. At least you could have named him Buffalo." Matsu said: "They have eaten all the buffalos."

Mr. Brosky no longer behaved in the gentlemanly manner as

before. He was laughing and with the help of the wheels of his chair was going here and there. Suddenly, he turned to Helmut and said: "Now, why did you name him 'earthworm'?" Helmut half got up and politely said: "Bookworm, Sir!" The employees mumbled, and Mr. Brosky said: "Yes, yes, excuse me." I said: "When he wants to sleep he has the habit of opening a book and putting it on his face so that he can sleep!" Mr. Brosky asked: "Is that true? Helmut do you actually sleep like that?" And he nodded. Mr. Brosky said: "What about Nooshka?" Matsu said: "This is a large polar bear." Mr. Brosky was hitting his fist on the table with laughter and joy, when he suddenly noticed the condition of his office. The employees had gathered around us. They were laughing and expressing opinions. Mr. Brosky braced himself and said: "Ladies and gentlemen, you know that something like this has never happened before, that we should become so disorderly and laugh and be joyous. All this is because five young people have come to this organisation. Wherever there are, young people are the source of joy and happiness. Today, I wanted to introduce them to each other, but since they have arrived last night, not only have they introduced themselves to each other, but also they have become so close that they have even given each other nicknames. When I suggested that affairs must be given to youngsters from the beginning, it was for this reason. Till now so many space scientists have gathered here. Honestly, have you ever seen them so sincere? Now, please return to your work." The employees went towards the door, and went out one by one. Mr. Brosky called Volkof.

Last night, Mr. Volkof brought each of us from the airport to our present residence. He was a thin man with a bony face and two thin lips that seem as two lines, because he has pressed them together so much. He seems to be nervous man. His manner with us was dry but polite. Mr. Volkof came to the room. Mr. Brosky looked at us with eagerness and smiling he said: "I'll trust you with these five treasures. Take care of them! We'll proceed as planned." Then he stood up by the door and shook hands with each of us and addressed us by the nicknames we had given each other. I felt that he wished he were our age and he could play with us and learn and study alongside us. We got into Mr. Volkof's car, which was a Station wagon with three rows of seats, and we headed towards our residence.

The place which since last night was given to us for some time was a white-coloured villa, with five bedrooms on the top floor. Opposite this large family house, was a small square with a statue placed in the middle. That night it seemed to be a quiet place.

We reached our residence. Victor opened the door. He was the cook and in charge of the house. Frederick said: "Dear Victor, what do we have for lunch? I am dying of hunger." Victor laughed and in broken English he said: "Come in first, then ask!" Frederick and Nooshka rushed to the kitchen. Mr. Volkof with the same stiff face and pressed lips came into the house and told us: "Since I brought you here separately last night, it was not possible to show you all the rooms. This is your recreation room. Here is a television set, a computer to play with, a chess set and sound systems, so that during your relaxation you would have everything."

This time I looked at the room carefully. The ceiling was very high and since the upstairs rooms were all around the banister it was circular, and the stairs spiralled upstairs. Mr. Volkof opened the door to another room and we followed him. Frederick and Nooshka came from the kitchen and entered the large room. "Here is your working room." Five computers bearing each of our names,

a number of diskettes and books and magazines were in place on each table, and a large bookshelf holding a number of valuable books was placed opposite our working tables. A rectangular table with five chairs stood on the other side of the room.

On one part of the wall a white-board with several magic-markers were seen. Another hall was for exercising. Various work-out equipment were placed here and there. Another, was the dining-room. And finally, a round table with five chairs was placed in the kitchen, which was separated from the dining-room by a few shelves.

Mr. Volkof then stood by the door and said: "Gentlemen, at six o'clock on the dot, you have a scientific excursion, be ready, I'll pick you up." He then opened the door and left.

Victor had made us a delicious lunch. Last night he helped us very much in naming ourselves. He didn't like some of our nick-names and he kept making us hot milk and cocoa. He kept insisting we find an appropriate name, and when he was thinking he would caress his large and full moustache, which was coming out of the sides of his face. When he laughed, his large stomach went up and down, under the white overall.

We were standing by the door of a large hall with beautiful and glorious carvings on the walls and ceiling (the center for Moscow Symphonic Orchestra). It had a very high ceiling, with windows high up there. The floor was covered with Persian carpets. The mirror-work on the ceiling and its colouring fascinated me. The men and women present were wearing formal clothes. Mr. Volkof had picked us up at 6 o'clock, and after a brief tour of the city, had brought us here to witness the performance of a few classical pieces.

Very soon, the doors opened and everyone, without any hurry, sat in his or her seat. Fifteen violin-players, three violin cellists and one pianist calmly and quietly appeared on the stage. People stood up and applauded them, and finally the gentleman who was the conductor entered the stage with a stick in his hand. Then they all bowed to the audience and sat down, and after a while they started playing. That night, I felt that art is the international language of humans. Because, no matter of what race, tribe or language they are, their hearts tremble and their emotions become delicate. When we returned, we discussed the music at our dining table. Helmut was of the opinion that the most difficult task in music was harmonising the sounds, therefore the conductor's job is very difficult. Victor was around the table constantly, removing the dishes, and expressed his opinion all the time. He said that it was difficult to play the accordion, and with his hands imitated playing the instrument. I expressed a wish that we could have a song of our own. Helmut said: "I play the guitar well." Nooshka said: "I have worked with the piano." Matsu said: "I can integrate music." Frederick said: "I know how to play the piano and the drums." As far as music was concerned, we were allright, although writing music is quite different from playing it, but there was no talk of writing a poem or a song. I volunteered to do that. Nooshka said: "We had better write several pieces of music, and discuss it with others. We shall be able to choose a good piece."

And it was decided that I should write a few poems for our melody so that we should all choose one of them. We rose to go to bed, and we thanked Victor for his delicious dinner. Caressing his moustache, he said: "Each of you has undertaken a task, am I a potato here?" Matsu said: "Oh! Victor, you should sing." Everybody burst out laughing. Even Victor, with his large tummy, was laughing hard. We went to the TV room and each of us talked to our families for a few minutes.

## 2

In a printed itinerary which Mr. Volkof had given us, it was written that this morning we were to visit an astrology and space center. We woke up very early. We took a shower, and we were in the middle of our breakfast, when Mr. Volkof arrived. He had a package in his hand. He said: "Hurry up and eat your breakfast. Here is some caviar! We have brought caviar from the Caspian Sea. A sea from whose natural resources we benefit jointly with Abtin's country." And as he was opening the box, he said: "Caviar is the best food in the world. It's full of vitamins." Then he took a little and with a little butter he spread it on a piece of bread and he started eating it quickly! We all worked up an appetite; and soon the container was empty. Helmut prodded me with his elbow and said: "Did you see whether he has teeth?!" Last night he and I had bet on whether Mr. Volkof had teeth or not. His lips were set in a way that one would think, he had no teeth. In any case, with his rapid eating we realised he had short teeth, and I had lost the bet.

When we sat in the car, Helmut said: "Our first research was on Mr. Volkof's teeth," and we both burst out laughing. Having traversed many roads and streets, we stopped in front of the entrance to a large area. A glass kiosk and a guard's post could be seen on two sides of a large gate. Mr. Volkof spoke to them in Russian. They spoke to their walkie-talkies, then the chains and the gate opened automatically. We entered a large area, which, except for a narrow road, was covered with grass. As we advanced, a high dome-shaped building appeared. The closer we came, the grander it seemed. Mr. Volkof stopped the car and we got off. Mr. Volkof stood by a metal staircase and said: "Well, we'll go up the steps." Nearly all of us screamed! So many steps!

Frederick said: "I thought that we would go to the moon with a rocket, I didn't know they had built a stairway to reach there." Helmut said: "Mr. Volkof, never mind us three! How do you want to bring these two bears and cow up

there!" The sound of our laughter attracted the attention of the gardeners and the guards. It seemed as though they were not accustomed to seeing jovial people.

Good-humouredly, Mr. Volkof said: "Why did you think I gave you all that caviar?! You're supposed to be young people. Go up!" And with a gesture of his finger he put me, Helmut, then Matsu, then Frederick and then Nooshka in a row one after the other and we started moving. I don't know how many stairs there were, but my knees had become numb. After a while Matsu said: "Look, Mr. Volkof's car seems so small." Frederick said: "Well, from this distance everything seems small, do you want to say you can even see with those two small peas?" Matsu said: "I can see better than you." As we were climbing, Mr. Volkof told us the history of this center for astrology, panting. Nooshka said: "Look at the times; a worm, a snake, and a rat are laughing at us." Finally the stairs came to an end and our shaky knees could relax. Then we passed through a narrow passage way. A big metal door slid open and a large hall appeared. The hall was a half circle and around it were large windows, and so much natural light had made the place very pleasant. A very large telescope was situated in the middle and its cylinder had penetrated the dome-shaped ceiling.

There was total silence. A few people wearing white overalls went around strange-looking equipment and were busy doing their work. A kind-faced man came forward and shook hands with Mr. Volkof. Some words were exchanged between them in Russian. Mr. Volkof, who was standing in front of the man very respectfully, said: "Gentlemen, Professor Ivanovich, the great scholar of astrology." One by one we went forward and shook hands with him, as we introduced ourselves. The professor was short and had white hair. Looking at us very carefully, he gestured towards the oval-shaped table in the corner of the room.

We sat on chairs around the table, but he started speaking, while he was standing.

"Hello, young scholars! Welcome to this research center. This is actually the place to study stars and celestial orbits. Here, we watch stars and satellites and by observing their whereabouts, we understand the situation of the earth's atmosphere. Sometimes we find stars, and sometimes we see the light of a star, which disintegrated years ago. At times we witness the destruction of a small planet and we await its consequences. The world of the cosmos is a special world, before you enter it you cannot discover its secrets. In addition, we sometimes make the preliminary calculations for satellites. Matsu asked: "Would you tell us a little about satellites?" Professor Ivanovich replied: "Well! Any object

that we throw upwards, after travelling a distance, eventually crashes to the earth. Well this is obvious, because of the earth's gravity. Now, the more power we throw it with, the faster it will go up and the faster it will come down.This means that speed will neutralize the earth's gravity for a few moments. Therefore, we conclude that speed is the secret of flight in space. Now, if we throw an object with a lot of power and very high speed to the farthest heights, and on its return we are able to establish the route of its movement with the curve of the earth with a calculated and set speed, with this speed, our object will stay in that height; precisely like the moon which rotates around us. For this reason, they call the satellites that are thrown to space, artificial moons.

Helmut asked: "On which orbits are the satellites you dispatch normally placed?" The professor replied: "Most of the satellites are placed at 20,000 to 35,900 kilometer orbits. Of course technology is constantly improving, so this information is for today not tomorrow! As you see the distances can be quite different."

I asked: "What is the ratio of their rotation with earth?" The professor responded: "In the height of 35,900 kilometers, they rotate the orbit every 24 hours. And it is interesting for you to know that in this height the rotation of the satellite is equal to our own earthly day and night. Therefore, if we dispatch a satellite from the angle of the equator to a distance of 35,900 kilometers from the earth, when we look at it through these telescopes, since its rotation is exactly as the earth's it seems to have zero speed, that is as a stationary star.

Matsu touched his glasses and said: "Do you mean that satellites orbit the earth in a circular manner?" The professor replies: "No! At different intervals their distance towards the earth differs and their rotation is elliptical.

Nooshka, who was taking notes all the time, raised his head and

asked: "Professor, what is the real reason for sending satellites around the earth?" Professor replied: "It could be for many reasons. For example, for information, communication," and after a moment of hesitation he said: "Most useful satellites are those used for communication. These satellites pick up the telephone or television waves that are sent by a transmitter in one spot on the earth, and transmits them back to another corner of the earth. Communication satellites are special types which are able to send the waves of several television channels and hundreds of telephone lines to other places.

Lately, the meteorological satellites have also advanced tremendously, which is extremely beneficial to humankind. They rotate on very high orbits and pick up various information. Meteorology experts are able to follow the routes of storms and whirlwinds and thus foretell their occurrence and save the inhabitants from harm. There also exist satellites which are used in navigation, and in tracing planes and ships. Another kind is used in the technology of resources on earth. These satellites take pictures, with green, red and infrared rays and they give precise specifications of underground resonance and transmit them to the earth."

Silence fell. Apparently we had no more specific questions. Satellites had taken us to the world of stars.

The professor invited us for refreshments and to look at the magazines and use the equipment and apparatus present there. All of us were anxious to look at the stars through the telescope, therefore we headed towards the equipment. Mr. Volkof ordered us not to change its focus. The professor did not go to tell Mr. Volkof off, but he said with indignation: "Excuse me, Mr. Volkof, these gentlemen are the young scientists of today and great scientists of tomorrow, they should be treated in a more polite manner." Then he faced us and said: "I beg you to use the equipment." Mr. Volkof apologized and said: "These young scientists as is the nature of their age are very active and naughty, if they get together they will not leave a brick on another brick."

We started studying the telescopes and the equipment there. When I was biting my sandwitch, I caught the kindness in the eyes of the professor who was looking at us. I said to myself: 'Will a day come when I also would be a great and kind scientist stretching across like him? Looking at the boundaries stretching across the skies has given him a vastness of horizon of thought and this is immensely valuable.'

After this, a diskette, a few books and a few articles and magazines were given to each of us under our own names. The professor said: "If you have any questions about these you can get in touch with me." Then as we said goodbye, he shook our hands. Here I registered the honour of shaking his hand in my mind for ever. We passed through the sliding door.

Helmut said: "Oh... you stairs... oh, you endless steps!" And we descended down the stairs. The children and I were thinking of the planets in the sky, the wonderful scenery we had seen through the telescopes for the first time which had left a special effect on us. Matsu suggested we compose the melody to our anthem. "Abtin you think of the words." Thus the narrow metal stairs became full of musical humming. Even after we got in the car, our thoughts were preoccupied with the satellites, on the way. There was silence and we were thinking. When we arrived at home, I was very happy. Home was a secure place, even if it was temporary. When Victor opened the door, we darted in like fiery bullets. Surprised, Victor pulled himself aside. Jokingly he said: "Has a dog followed you?" Just at that moment Mr. Volkof came into the house. Victor was shameful and went into the kitchen, but we laughed loudly. We washed our hands and face and sat around the table to be served by Victor. Calmly and patiently, Victor went on with his work. Nooshka asked: "Victor, do you want to kill us with hunger?" Mr. Volkof wrote the next day's itinerary on the white board in the study-room, and said goodbye and left.

Victor brought us lunch. We were not satisfied, and wanted more. He brought us seconds and Frederick and Nooshka wanted more for the third time. Victor said: "The way you two eat, I am afraid the food stuff will be finished for humankind. Nooshka said: "Don't you know that we are supposed to go to the moon and breed sheep, and grow potatoes and wheat?"

Amazed, Victor cleaned his hands on his apron and said: "I know both sheep rearing and planting potatoes and wheat," then beggingly he said: "Take me with you." As we did not expect such an offer, we burst out laughing, and Victor with his hanging moustache went to the kitchen. We didn't want him to think we had teased him and feel hurt.

## 3

Since three days we had been waking up early in the morning. After eating breakfast we would get behind the computers and we would work hard.

On the first day we realized that the subjects they had given us to research were different for each of us. Therefore, we could not rely on the minds or thoughts of others. Sometimes we had to read until late into the night. At times, the problems seemed unsolvable to us and we had to get in touch with the professor and ask for guidance. Most of the time he would ask our opinion in the end, and we would realise that it was quite serious. There was silence in the study room all the time. Sometimes we would go to the kitchen for a break, we would pour tea or coffee and bring it to our table. But Victor always announced lunchtime. He would call us twice, and if we did not show at the table, he would make us eat our food cold. For this reason with the first call, we tried to sit at the table. During lunch or dinner, we would tell each other of interesting things we had come across, so that all of us could experience those problems. Whenever there were differences of opinion, Victor would come with a big spoon and would hit it on the table and would say: "Eat first and argue later, because you'll miss the good taste of my food." And at times he would turn the music so loud that we would have to ask him to turn it down, and we would promise not to talk any more.

Whenever we wrote out the problems and solved them with each other's help, we would rejoice. Sometimes we would find the answer through two different solutions, and each would want to convince the other. It was the third day and I had finished half of the research asked of me. My eyes were burning with fatigue. I was sitting behind my desk, drowned in my thoughts. I took off my glasses so that my eyes could rest. After a while my eyes turned towards the door. From where I was looking, I saw Victor sitting on the steps and observing us. He seemed very sad and quiet. I put on my glasses, so that I could see him better. He was bored. Laughing, I made a face. He got up and took a chair and came and sat opposite me. He asked me: "What happened to all that noise and happiness? How much homework do you do?" I said: "Victor! We have come here for this. This is the biggest goal in our life." The rest stared at us and said: "Hush, hush." Victor looked at them and said: "My God, we cannot say two words! I am a poor soul! I am dying of boredom." The children looked up from their books and computers. They said: "Victor is right." Victor continued: "It's been three days since some of you have taken a shower. Almost none of you have exercised. I'm not a potato here."

Matsu and Helmut burst out laughing. I said: "Do you want to play football for an hour after dinner?" The others nodded. I said: "Victor will play with us." Victor responded: "I have not played football all my life." Nooshka said: "It's obvious with your big tummy." Frederick said: "Look who's talking!" And we laughed. Victor was delighted. He picked up his chair and left. That night he announced dinner half an hour early. Matsu looked at his watch and said: "Naughty Victor!" We went out of the house, after dinner. Nearby we found a suitable ground, and drew lines to mark the goals. We chose partners. Nobody wanted Victor, but I chose him. Whispering, Victor said: "I don't know anything. I'm afraid you'll lose." I said: "You only stand by the goal, you needn't do anything." Soon our game started.

Nobody could score a goal against us, since Victor's huge tummy had filled the goal, and thus we won. The game was good exercise for us, and made our blood flow. We became alive and made Victor lively. When we were going up the stairs to our rooms to go to bed, Victor pointed his finger at us, in a warning manner and said: "Tomorrow morning, all of you must bathe." Matsu said: "He's our mother!"

A few days had passed. I felt I had reached a logical conclusion relating to my research. I was very happy. I started typing the whole thing. After that I reread the result. Although it had taken a lot of time, I was satisfied with the result. I asked for Mr. Volkof's e-mail address and I e-mailed my report and result to him. Matsu e-mailed his report, immediately after me. Frederick said: "I sent mine this morning." Nooshka was finishing his typing, Helmut was still in his books and was going from this book to that. When he realized that all of us had finished our work, he seemed nervous, and this delayed his work.

The next day all of us, except for Helmut, were free. We went to the exercise room and exercised on the machines. We watched TV and discussed the song we wanted to make. Helmut was still labouring. Mr. Volkof telephoned and asked: "What has happened to Helmut's report? Until I receive the last piece of work, I cannot take you out." We went to the study room in the afternoon to help Helmut, when we realized that he had finished his work, but he was too fussy to part with it. Before he knew it we faxed his report to Mr. Volkof. Helmut was angry and he kept swearing and cursing under his breath, but we were bored and wanted some recreation. Mr. Volkof informed us that the next day we would go to a beautiful forest park.

Over supper Nooshka told us how beautiful the forest was that we were supposed to visit. He said: "It has so many beautiful sceneries that one becomes confused." Victor said: "We will fish there and we'll grill the fish." Nooshka said: "Mr. Volkof may not let you come." Victor came to our table and begged us to take him along no matter what.

When Mr. Volkof came to fetch us, he saw Victor dressed and ready to go. Surprised he said: "Why have you gotten dressed up? You're not supposed to go with us." Victor said: "I've prepared the fishing rods and picnic basket. We want to fish and then grill the fish. In all of Russia no can catch fish like me." Mr. Volkof shook his head. Suddenly, all of us surrounded him and asked him to let Victor accompany us. He gave Victor a dirty look, but soon he stopped frowning, especially when we came onto the beautiful, green route towards the forest. Victor was so happy that he could not sit still. He, alone, had occupied a row of seats and if he had not been afraid of Mr. Volkof he would now be singing with his disastrous voice. We passed the fir trees and came to an artificial lake. A shed which was made of wood and straws and looked very simple but beautiful, was close by. The car doors opened and we jumped out as prisoners freed from a cage. Mr. Volkof kept shouting and saying things. But, after so many days of sitting in front of computers and being lost in books and articles, we had no patience to listen to anybody in this paradise on earth. We undressed and jumped into the cool water of the lake. With a frothed up mouth, Mr. Volkof kept walking about. Then we saw Victor roll-up his trousers and start fishing. We came out of the water. Victor caught a few fish. Frederick said he knew how to grill fish as the Red-Indians do. So it was decided that all of us should help Victor in cleaning the fish, and Frederick took a thin stick and with that he cooked the fish over the fire. Inside the shed, Victor had spread a blanket, and had set a paper plate full of salad and paper cups filled with soft-drinks, for each of us. When we were eating lunch, Mr. Volkof said: "You worried me so much that I lost my appetite."

"To let Mr. Brosky know how difficult my mission was, I've taken pictures of all your naughty moves and moments." We were delighted, because we thought we had no souvenir of our trip to the forest. We asked him to give us copies of the photos. It was four o'clock. Mr. Volkof kept calling for us in the woods. I had climbed a tree and was fighting with Matsu who had also climbed a tree. We were throwing pinnacles at each other. Hearing Mr. Volkof's voice that was trembling with anger, we came down, found the other three and headed towards the car. The sky was growing dark. When we reached home, all of us except for Mr. Volkof who was driving, were asleep. When I woke up the next morning, there was the sound of music coming from downstairs. Happy and gay, Victor was humming a Russian tune which was being broadcast on the radio.

We had just finished breakfast, when the doorbell rang. Victor opened the door and Mr. Volkof jumped in. "Why aren't you

ready? You have an appointment today." He had told us last night, but since we were sleepy we had not understood. We went to our rooms immediately and got dressed and took our books. As I was coming down the stairs, I caught Victor giving Mr. Volkof a dirty look. He could not contain himself and grumbled: "Whenever you take them for these meetings, the house becomes silent for a week. You give them so much homework that I get bored." Mr. Volkof squeezed his short teeth and said: "I believe they've come from their country to talk to you. Is that right?"

All of us got into the car with hanging heads. Frederick returned to the house to tell Victor not to make the meat sauce too hot. The car had not started yet and Mr. Volkof gave each of us an envelope. The envelopes contained the pictures of day before. Thus the dry and stiff atmosphere of the car became more relaxed. When we saw the pictures, we realised how wild we had acted yesterday without knowing it. Mr. Volkof asked: "Have you seen the picture I took of you on the top of the tree?" When I saw it, my tummy ached with laughter. Not only did our faces look like those of crazy people, but our expressions were like those who had lost their heads. But when Mr. Volkof said that he wanted to show the pictures to Mr. Brosky, all of us changed our attitude and sat quietly.

We passed the roads and the car stopped in front of a large gate with iron grates. Once more, Volkof spoke with the guard in Russian and after a while they let us enter. Mr. Volkof stopped the car in the parking lot and another car, which was a Jeep station, appeared. The driver opened the door and we got in and entered the area. The pine trees and winding road reminded me of yesterday's trip in the beautiful forest park.

## 4

The row of pine trees, standing straight and stiff like soldiers, ended. A white building appeared in front of us. Inside the building there was silence. Only the sound of our footsteps echoed. The floor of the building was covered by a white, shiny stone.

We passed through wide passageways. At times we could hear people talking behind closed doors, but we encountered no one. Mr. Volkof stood by a door. He knocked several times and then opened the door. It was a large hall of glass closets. Inside them were lots of small rockets built as models, there were also a number of pictures of small rockets, satellites and various people. We were so delighted to see the small satellites that we left Mr. Volkof and the rest and stood looking at them behind the glass closets. Their size was very miniscule, but they contained all the parts. I wished they would hand them to me so that I could play with them for hours. Suddenly Mr. Volkof put his hand on our shoulders and said: "It's not right to keep a great scholar waiting." Mr. Nicola Petronovich had a serious face, but he wanted us to understand that his intentions were friendly. He shook our hands and welcomed us. Then he took us to see the rockets. "We have the most primitive and the most advanced in the closets. You can have a look at them, then we'll start our new discussion." After we had scrutinised the rockets and come back to stand next to him, Mr. Petronovich took us to another room which had a few chairs and computers. Then he said: "What do you think is

Van Allen

the most effective element in starting any activity?" Frederick answered: "To know what is our goal." Helmut said: "Our planning should be compatible with our principles and our capabilities." Mr. Petronovich said: "First we need knowledge. We should know enough to enable us to plan." Then he drove his wheelchair towards a table on which there was a computer.

He pressed a button at random and the words "Van Allen" appeared on the screen. Professor Nicola, then turned to us and said: "Therefore, above all, we know that information and its retrieval is one of the most important and basic elements that exists in the present century. To understand anything we need background information, and among all the different media today, I am talking about receiving information via satellite.

"We have to remember that no matter how diligent or active our mind may be, it is not able to contain more than a certain amount of information. Therefore, we need to have a tank to store the information on which we are working. We need to constantly update our information and preserve it, in order to benefit from it at the right time. For example, these very words that appeared on the monitor's screen accidentally – 'Van Allen...' At the beginning of the space era, with the information received from satellites, they discovered an amassed radiation which appeared like a belt within a distance from the earth. They called this belt 'Van Allen', and they filled the information here (he pointed to the computer). Do you have a question?"

Frederick said: "Professor, I have a question about the process of receiving information and measuring something from a long distance." The professor who was tall and had a hairless head, looked at Frederick thoughtfully and said: "We obtain such information by telemetric equipment. This is a long distance measuring device, whose information is relayed to the earth via satellite. This equipment is made of a cassette player and a radio. As the satellite moves, it registers various information in the form of waves and short and small signals. When we are faced with a problem in researching the situation in that area, we send the question code which has previously been placed on the memory of that apparatus through special waves and send it to the satellite. First, the tape reverses itself automatically, exactly like our own tape recorders. Then you can research any information and make use of it on earth. I asked where the power for the satellites come from. The professor looked at me and said: "Look, all the equipment inside the satellite, like the recorder, the radio transmitter and so on... need electricity. It is not possible to use ordinary batteries, since they cannot be recharged. For this reason, solar batteries are used since there is always sunshine in space."

Matsu asked: "What are solar-batteries made off?" Professor Nicola answered. "From a number of tiny silicon cells in each of which a weak electrical current is produced through the rays of the sun." Nooshka asked: "In which part of the satellite are the batteries placed?" The professor said: "Normally on the wings placed on each side of the satellite." Then he opened the door of a cabinet and took out a few small satellites and he described their different parts. I picked one of them up and in my imagination took it to space. I sat inside it. The session was finished, when I came to myself, and I had no idea what had been said. The professor gave us an assignment on a thorough research on information gathering. Separate books and thesis were handed to us plus the instruction about how to use them in different diskettes. Since the professor's students had come into the room for their class, Mr. Volkof took us to a café and we each had a piece of pastry and a soft drink. There, I was able to see a few of the Moskovites.

When we got home and Victor opened the door, he stepped back as usual, so that if we ran in like bullets he would not get hurt. But we entered like gentlemen. Surprised, Victor, drying his hands with his apron, said: "Is today a special day?" Frederick said: "Yes, because Mr. Volkof was generous and bought us drinks. Consequently, we shall not come to you for food for one hour." Victor asked again: "The place where you went to visit did they give you homework, as well?" We laughed, since we knew he was worried about his own loneliness. All of us said: "Lots!" And Victor, with his droopy moustache, sulkily went into the kitchen.

When I sat behind my desk to start working, I realised that Professor Nicola had given me all the key elements for the research. He had made my work easy, but he had asked me to find a way to the information, aside from what had existed up to now. The new plan needed much studying and thinking, and this thought became a part of my existence.

In the evenings, an hour after supper, we would play football. Victor, who was very popular with his large belly, recently had become snobbish and genuinely thought he was a good player. We would not break his heart, because we knew that he would spend his days for the love of football at night. Matsu had made a piece of music for our song, but since the melody was not good, we did not accept it. I found a new system for gathering information, but I was dubious. I called Professor Nicola. He listened carefully and after some thought, he said it was not a bad plan, but needed more studying. He said: "You must outline the frame of the plan and write a complete programme for it. Then you should report to me." His concession was a victory for me. Now, I saw my objective more clearly. I started studying and researching it...

Matsu had finished his plan, and was typing it rapidly so that he could give it to Mr. Volkof. Without showing anything, I felt I had to work faster to finish my work.

Three days later, we had all given our work in. Helmut stayed up most nights so that he would not keep everybody waiting like the last time.

Mr. Volkof extended Mr. Brosky's good wishes to us and the fact that he had expressed satisfaction with our progress. Then he said he would take us to the fun-fair. Nooshka said: "There they have strange equipment and it is full of excitement and laughter."

Each of us had a memory of the fun-fair in our own country. It was five o'clock in the afternoon. We dressed and awaited Mr. Volkof. Mr. Volkof was half an hour late. As he opened the door, Victor who had become more confident, objected to Mr. Volkof's delay in Russian, which made Mr. Volkof angry; pressing his lips

together harder, so that their thin line appeared thinner. Victor who wished to come on our excursion, became upset at his own untimely outburst and suddenly with a smile said: "A man must know the reason for his anger or sadness. To live happily is a decision. Whatever we have is from joy!" He said these words with literary feelings, for this reason at first we became quiet and listened. Was it really Victor? All of a sudden, tears started running down our faces from laughter. Mr. Volkof was laughing in a manner that seemed as if he had been robbed of this blessing for years. His thin face opened-up and his cheeks folded like an accordion. The sweet speech of Victor scored a point and Mr. Volkof allowed him to join us. Helmut went to his side and said: "You naughty man, you steal our words and pretend to be a philoso pher!" Victor fetched his coat in a hurry and said: "Run, kids, Mr. Volkof might change his mind any minute." Mr. Volkof was still laughing in the car, and he had put on a tape with very loud music,

but we said nothing out of respect. We watched the streets and tried not to hear the music. All of a sudden, Victor said: "Excuse me. I cannot stop myself, but this tape has an ugly sound. Would it be possible for you to play one of AQUA's tapes?"

We all looked at him with surprise. Matsu had bent down and was shaking with laughter. Mr. Volkof said "What tape?" Victor said hesitantly: "I think it is called Aqua." It was a hilarious scene. Mr. Volkof was looking at Victor in the rear-view mirror. He said: "You know the new tape? And you are repeating the words of the new generation. Tell me, Victor, have you learned to use the computer as well?" He said: "No, sir. But they're supposed to teach me, so that when they go to the their country I would be able to send them a fax." All of us tried to laugh silently so that Victor would not lose his confidence. He suddenly said: "I would like to go to the moon with them and rear sheep and grow wheat there, and at the same time cook for them. Because they will get sick if they eat other food..."

It was a delightful night. Victor rode on the electric car, like us. He went around the park with play-trains and entertained us with his strange talk. The most important point was that he taught us not to be afraid of Mr. Volkof anymore and become friendly with him. He had found a place for himself in Mr. Volkof's heart.

## 5

Exactly at 8: 30 a.m. Mr. Volkof honked the horn of his car. We opened the door quickly so that we could start our visit together. Frederick and Nooshka were arguing with Victor over the menu for lunch. Victor came up to the car like a person to whom one owes money and said to Mr. Volkof : "After each visit they have to do homework for one week. They are so silent that I become bored. Instead at the dining table they all talk together." Mr. Volkof said: "Try to learn the computer so that you can fax letters to it too." Victor rushed home and brought a tape back for us. Then he winked at us to say: you owe me one!

Travelling now would be more pleasant with this tape. On the way, Nooshka and Matsu were betting on the ending of a film they had seen years ago. Helmut and Frederick carried on their never-ending argument about the best sports shoes whose sole could make walking lighter. Mr. Volkof listened to our favourite song and I, while watching the outside view, liked to travel inside myself and evaluate what I'd done so far and if my yesterday was like the day before? Whether my activities had been towards my goal? Whether I was satisfied with my progress? What my family was doing now in Iran? And my classmates? All of a sudden I felt very homesick.

When the car stopped we all came to our senses. Again, we had been stopped in front of a 'STOP' sign. And again Mr. Volkof's talking with the guards and their asking permission from the

authorities was repeated. This time we did not have to wait for long. The barrier was lifted and we were let in. A large official building appeared with its roof top full of satellite dishes and television antennas and communication screens.

When Mr. Volkof parked his car in the permitted area, he said: "Today is another mysterious day. I hope you will take advantage of this visit, fully. Today, you will visit Professor Krokansha; he is a great man." Saying this, he led the way as always and we followed him through many halls. This place was crowded, noisy and busy. We stopped at a large hall in which there were four rows of tables and some people were sitting behind computer monitors. Mr. Volkof was looking for Mr. Krokansha frantically, and each person to whom he asked about his whereabouts, would look around and say: "He was here right now. Where did he go?" We understood that he must be a light and fast-moving person, who suddenly disappears. Finally Mr. Volkof found him while he was talking to a number of people all at once, and walking very quickly. He had white, wild hair, and was wearing thick glasses. Almost running, Mr. Volkof reached him. He waited until the professor had finished talking. But he went to another room and his followers including Mr. Volkof disappeared from our view. After a while, Mr. Volkof brought him toward us. Smiling, he asked us: "So you are the young scholars? Well, well..." And he shook hands with us. We introduced ourselves, then he ran to the next room, and we followed him. It was a fairly large room in which there were a few computers and television sets. He ordered us to bring chairs for ourselves from the opposite hall. After we had settled in our chairs, he scratched his head, and his wild hair became more ruffled. He started thus: "I am not in a habit of talking too much, I shall tell you the gist of the matter, the rest is up to you. Our goal is to prolong the space research or it is better that I should say establishing a permanent station in space, to be able to carry on sensitive research in it. Also it should be a place for stopping over for astronauts coming for research from other countries beyond the atmosphere. And, of course a place for watching and controlling the earth.

"The day we made this decision, many people laughed at us. This seemed like a fairy-tale. But science can change a fairy-tale into reality. Like the large legendary birds which have now become helicopters and airplanes or rockets... To realise our dream, we were very persistent. We failed, experienced, failed and tried again... and finally we succeeded.

"We sent the first Saliot to space as the primary step in this experience..." He pressed a few buttons on the computer. The image of Saliot appeared. "Saliot is a cylinder with a length of twenty meters, and its weight equals twenty tons. It was thrown into space in 1971. Its power is acquired by two solar batteries, which are placed in its front and back. On one side there is a hinge and hook which is the place of attachment for Soyuz." (After that he pressed a few more buttons and the picture of a man appeared). He added: "The first flight of Saliot ended with the heroic death of Colonel Vladimir Markof."

Helmut asked: "Did he really die?" We all laughed. Dr. Krokansha laughed too and said: "Yes, death is the only task that we all carry out completely."

Matsu murmured under his breath: "He shamed us."

Professor Krokansha continued: "But on its way back the space craft ran into some difficulty and crashed. Of course Markof could have jumped out with a parachute, but he stayed back and lost his life. After that other things happened. The cosmonauts of Soyuz 2, 3, 4 and 5 made some rendezvous in space. The passengers of Saliot II were able to stay in space for 24 hours and work, which was the best record of a sojourn in space up to that date.

"Three more Saliots were sent into space until 1975, among which Saliot IV was more successful than the others. The cosmonauts of Saliot XVII extended their stay to thirty days. And the passengers of Saliot XVIII broke the record and stayed for 63 days. By this time, the Americans had also completed their successful work on 'Sky Lab'... In this programme, three teams of astronauts met in the space station." Frederick asked: "How was it that before sending man into space, they did not experiment with animals?"

Professor Krokansha explained that on 3rd November 1978 the Sputnik II space craft was put in the earth's orbit carrying a dog called Lyka. This should have been done before sending man into space, since the metal alloy of a space craft and its resistance in space could have been measured, but humans and living things in general have a different measure of resistance towards pressure, waves and radiation. In any case, humans are made of flesh, blood, bones and nerves, and are very sensitive. The pressure induced at the time of launch is very great.

The professor, then pressed his fingers on some buttons on the TV set and some images appeared. And for the first time we

saw the Mir Station from different angles. Two Russian cosmonauts were in it. We became so excited by seeing it that all of us got up from our chairs in order to see in better. Mir was floating in space and its automatic systems were sending information to earth. The time of our visit with the professor was up, but we were still fascinated and flabbergasted by watching the Mir Station. The professor said: "Well, I am happy to have seen you." And he shook hands with each of us. He lent us a few books on the use of computers in space, variance in radiation and he also gave us some diskettes on speed and its measurement.

As he was leaving, he put his hair in order with his hand and said: "I'll see you in the Mir Station in a few days." Then he smiled and left us in the world of the Mir Station.

When we were returning home, there was complete silence in the car. Suddenly Nooshka asked: "Mr. Volkof, when are we going to the Mir Station?" Mr. Volkof laughed and said: "This was the last session of a lesson in theory. You have to prepare your bodies for space, which is void of gravity. I mean weightlessness. You have to learn that well too, to reach the last stage."

We were sitting around the table and having lunch. Mr. Volkof had gone to bring a person to repair Nooshka's computer. Having seen the Mir Station in the blue sky, which was attractive to us, the discussion about it was very hot. Frederick said: "Not even in my dreams did I think that I would go so high in the sky." I said: "One day our teacher for composition asked me, what I wanted to be in the future, and I said, 'a pilot'. Asked why, I said, 'Because I like to see everything from high up'." Nooshka said: "I wanted to become a confectioner." We all laughed. Helmut said: "I wanted to be a merchant. When I was in kindergarten I would catch frogs and sell them to the kids. It was a good trade."

But now, we were all thinking of a great dream. To go up to

the highest level, one that is beyond the atmosphere. As Victor was serving us, he would pause to enter our discussion. Suddenly, he said: "Do you really want to get into these jalopies and go to the moon?" Nooshka said: "They're not jalopies anymore, they've been repaired." Benignly, Victor said "Take me with you. I'll cook for you and wash the dishes, so that you'll be comfortable."

Mr. Volkof entered with the expert he had brought for repair. Good-humouredly he said: "The sound of your laughter can be heard on the other side of Moscow, what has happened?" I said: "Victor wants to come to the moon with us." Mr. Volkof faced Victor and said: "They will not be going to the moon, they will be turning around the earth. If you go with them you'll get dizzy and fall down." Victor, who realised we were kidding him, laughed loudly.

We did not go to work until Nooshka's computer was fixed. We wanted to start work together, but we felt anxious about it. Finally, Mr. Volkof announced that the computer was fixed. Nooshka sat behind it and bowed his head in satisfaction, and we all started to work.

This time the work was more research oriented and we needed a more comprehensive encyclopedia. Therefore, I called Mr. Volkof and he promised to provide it for us the next day. In the meantime, I started studying the Mir Station. The dream of living in the earth's orbit had filled my mind.

Matsu said: "It is useless. I cannot understand many of the terminologies." Nooshka said: "Same here." Frederick got up to go to the kitchen, and he said: "If he brings us one book, we cannot all use it." Then he went to make himself a chocolate milk. I became tempted and Nooshka and Matsu joined me. He pointed to Helmut and said: "Look, just like a bookworm. What a name we've given him!" Not even our laughter could make him lift his head. When we had nothing to do we would play around. So, when Frederick took off his socks we threw it at each other. They smelled very bad. All our socks were smelling bad, but Frederick's were something else! Victor's shouting got nowhere. Frederick who was dying with laughter, could not get his socks back from us. We went to the study and hit it at Helmut's face. He seemed as though he was in another world, and suddenly came to and shouted: "What's happened?" Then he held his nose and said: "Oh! Oh! What a horrible smell." And he threw it at my head. Thus the place was in total chaos. All of a sudden, the socks fell on the lamp, and Victor came to the room grumbling. Seeing our laughter he started laughing. But suddenly he said: "You are foolish scholars. Presently, this socks will steam and suffocate us all." He was right. The smell of the socks had filled the room completely! Nooshka brought Victor's broom and hit the socks. The socks fell from the lamp and we cheered. The place was so disorderly that Victor kept saying thanks to Mr. Volkof, because he constantly brought us work and made us sit calmly and quietly on the chairs. Suddenly, we remembered our song. Tonight since we could not work on our research, we could at least work on our song. The composers gathered and practiced. I was in charge of the words, but at that time poetic blood was not boiling in my veins.

Early the next morning, Mr. Volkof brought three encyclopedias and three boxes of chocolates. Mr. Brosky had sent them and had not forgotten Victor.

Nooshka said: "I wish you had brought five. Now with these three books, we'll get into a fight." Mr. Volkof laughed and said: "I don't think you'll fight together. It is better for you to get used to sharing tools. This is a kind of life too." As he was leaving, we asked him to say hello to Mr. Brosky and thank him for the chocolates.

All of us ate our chocolates soon after, except for Helmut. He was very stingy. He ate some of his chocolates and looked at the rest. He did not have the heart to eat it all. He wrote his name on the chocolate bar with a magic marker and put it in the fridge. A few hours later while we were working, we heard Helmut's scream. We rushed to the kitchen. The fridge door was open and Helmut was very angry. He said: "I don't know which impolite person has eaten my chocolate. I had even written my name on it." Frederick and Nooshka looked at each other. Helmut said: "No good, pot-bellies! You could have at least asked my

permission." Matsu said: "A gluttonous cow and a greedy bear!"

Thus the tumult was finished and we went back to work. Studying the Mir Station had an extra attraction because we could see it through its pictures. Also, we were supposed to experience all the details of the flight with our senses; therefore, we had to know it well by heart.

One week passed. My work was finished, typed and ready for the review of Mr.Brosky and Professor Krokansha. The others were more or less ready too. We were all very excited, since this was our last work in theory. From then on we would have fun with exercise and going to the weightless room. To help Helmut finish, everyone was typing one part of his work. He was grumbling angrily.

In the evening we called Mr. Volkof and gave him the good news that Helmut's work was finally finished. He told us to wait for him tomorrow; we would go to the weightless room.

After dinner and playing football, we still had a lot of energy. We did not feel sleepy, and we were excited. Nice, fast music was playing. After we went to our bedrooms, we felt like a game of pillow-fight. I don't know how many hours we played. Victor, hitting himself on the head, came and took the pillows from us. The room was full of feathers.

When we reached the Space Building of Moscow, it was 9 o'clock. Since we did not feel shy of Mr. Volkof any more, we started singing. The notes of our song were almost ready. Still some parts needed review. Some parts of the melody were not quite right. I wanted it to have a little eastern intonation, and they accepted it. Therefore, at the time of writing the notes, they asked me to come and listen to it.

In the weightlessness section, we arrived at a place for changing clothes. When the person in charge saw us, he told us we could not all go in together. Therefore, Frederick and Nooshka went in and Helmut, Matsu and myself waited. The special tailor for cosmonauts took measurements for the particular clothes. As he explained, he had to sew ten layers together, since the direct radiation of sun is highly hazardous to the human body. Two hours passed, then they came out. Helmut, Matsu and myself changed clothes. First we entered a ball, then a container which had a large oval glass door, which closed tightly like the door of a refrigerator. Our instructor, Mr. Veronick, kept giving us special instructions. First he gave us a few exercises and then he took us to the small room and he closed the door. There I felt that the earth was not under my feet, just like the times I swam in the sea or the pool, but even more weightless. Matsu's feet were up and his head down, the two of us were dying of laughter. Matsu said: "Now I understand why those two were so vivacious when they came to get their clothes." We had a lot of fun that day. Matsu and I somersaulted and slept in mid-air and lots of other things that made us forget about the earth. Contrary to other scientists, Mr. Veronick was very sporty, strong and joyful. On saying goodbye, he shook my hands in such a way that my fingers were stuck together for a while. In his opinion, we were a bunch of weaklings, who had exercised little, and he had to build our bodies. Therefore, we had to have exercises for one week straight, in the mornings and afternoons. Then he touched the muscles of my legs and said: "These legs have not even walked. And the body of your two fat friends are no good."

At six o'clock the next day, Mr. Veronick attired in a sweat suit, was standing at the door. We queued up to the sound of his whistle, and almost running we went towards the side street. Victor was watching us, aghast. We came home at 8, tired but jovial and fresh. Victor had set a large breakfast for us. We were

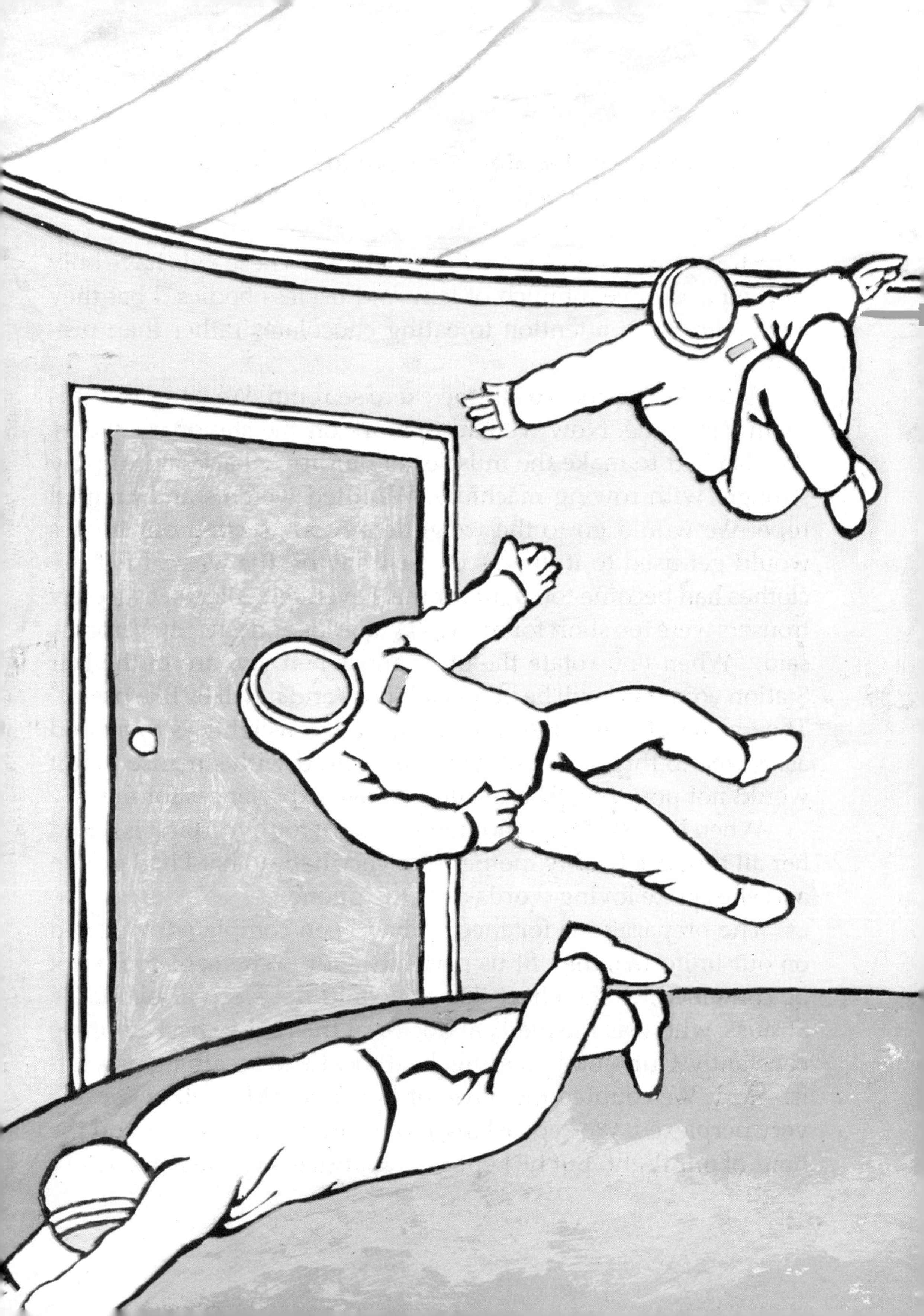

hungry and thirsty. We almost devoured anything edible on the table. Victor brought us seconds and grumbled: "Have you come from a famine?"

Mr. Veronick told Victor: "Let them eat. These kids have only studied and have a bunch of lazy and useless bodies. I bet they have paid more attention to eating chocolates rather than proteins."

After that he took us to the exercise room. We had used this room very little. Now we had to work on the stationary cycles. We also had to make the muscles of our arms, back and tummy stronger with rowing machines. We lifted weights and jumped rope. We would go to the weightless room, so that our bodies would get used to it. It was the last day of the week. I felt my clothes had become too tight for me. I even felt taller, because my trousers were too short for me. I felt vigorous and gay. Mr. Veronick said; "When you rotate the orbit and when you are in the Mir Station your food will be in special tubes and it will be like paste." Then he handed me a glass of water in the weightless room and asked me to throw it at Matsu, we realised with surprise that it would not pour out. These were strange experiences for me.

When I talked to my mother that night for five minutes, I told her all this, briefly. My mother was very happy that I had grown and she spoke loving words over the phone.

The preparations for the trip had been completed. We tried on our uniforms, they fit us perfectly. Our excitement could not be contained, to the effect that we could not sleep at night. Dr. Strauss, who was the medical doctor of the flight, checked us up constantly. Our blood pressure, heart beat and breathing was satisfactory. We counted the days for our flight. Mr. Volkof became very perplexed. We kept asking him to announce the day and the hour of our flight. But he kept saying until everything was ready he could not do that. And finally that day arrived, the day that was like no other in my life.

## 6

Mr. Volkof took us to see Mr. Brosky. Mr. Brosky shook our hands very intimately. I remembered the first day that I had seen him in the same room, and his surprise at the friendship of five young men from five different countries. Now he was friendly with us too. We were sitting around the table and watching his blue eyes and his hanging double chin.

He said: "Young men, all your work, research, activities and innovations have been registered here in a collection for each of you. We have constantly studied them. Although your thoughts were not alike, they were successful. Scholars such as Professor Ivanovich, Professor Nicola Petronovich, Professor Krokansha and Mr. Veronick have written their opinion for you. I think that a successful person is one whose today is different from his yesterday and tomorrow. I feel that since the day I saw you, you have improved greatly mentally, physically, scientifically and in your thoughts. We have done everything in our power, but this is not the end of the road. Your real research will be in space and the Mir Station. We expect you to find a solution for our planet, its revival, and the well-being of this mother of all mothers. I expect you to take an eternal step for your generation." And he brought the glass globe to the table, which had attracted me the first day when I wanted to touch it. He made it rotate and said: "This is our Earth, belonging to all of us, we all live together on it, animals, plants, beasts and we rotate around the sun. You should look at it in such a light. Tomorrow is the day that you sit in the rocket and will fly on the wings of science, to go to another temporary home. Your mind is young and resourceful. You must help to save humanity and our environment."

My eyes fell on the glass globe and I was taken to my childhood and my coloured marbles...(Suddenly I realised the meeting was over). At the time of saying goodbye, the kids called each other with the nicknames we had chosen for each other, blind mouse... polar bear... rattle snake... black cow... bookworm, and Mr. Brosky laughed loudly and was delighted.

That night, I called my mother. Her voice was trembling. She was a strong woman, and I felt strong next to her. She told me she would pray for me. I spoke to my sister as well, she was also worried.

We were at the Moscow Space Centre, at 4 a.m. the next morning. All our teachers and trainers were present. Mr. Brosky gave us the last minute tips. The reporters and TV crews were present with their cameras. They were asking us to send a message to the young people of the world, I was quite excited. I did not know what to do. The cosmonauts' suit was not that comfortable. Mr. Brosky came to me hurriedly and said: "The president of your country wants to talk to you." My heart

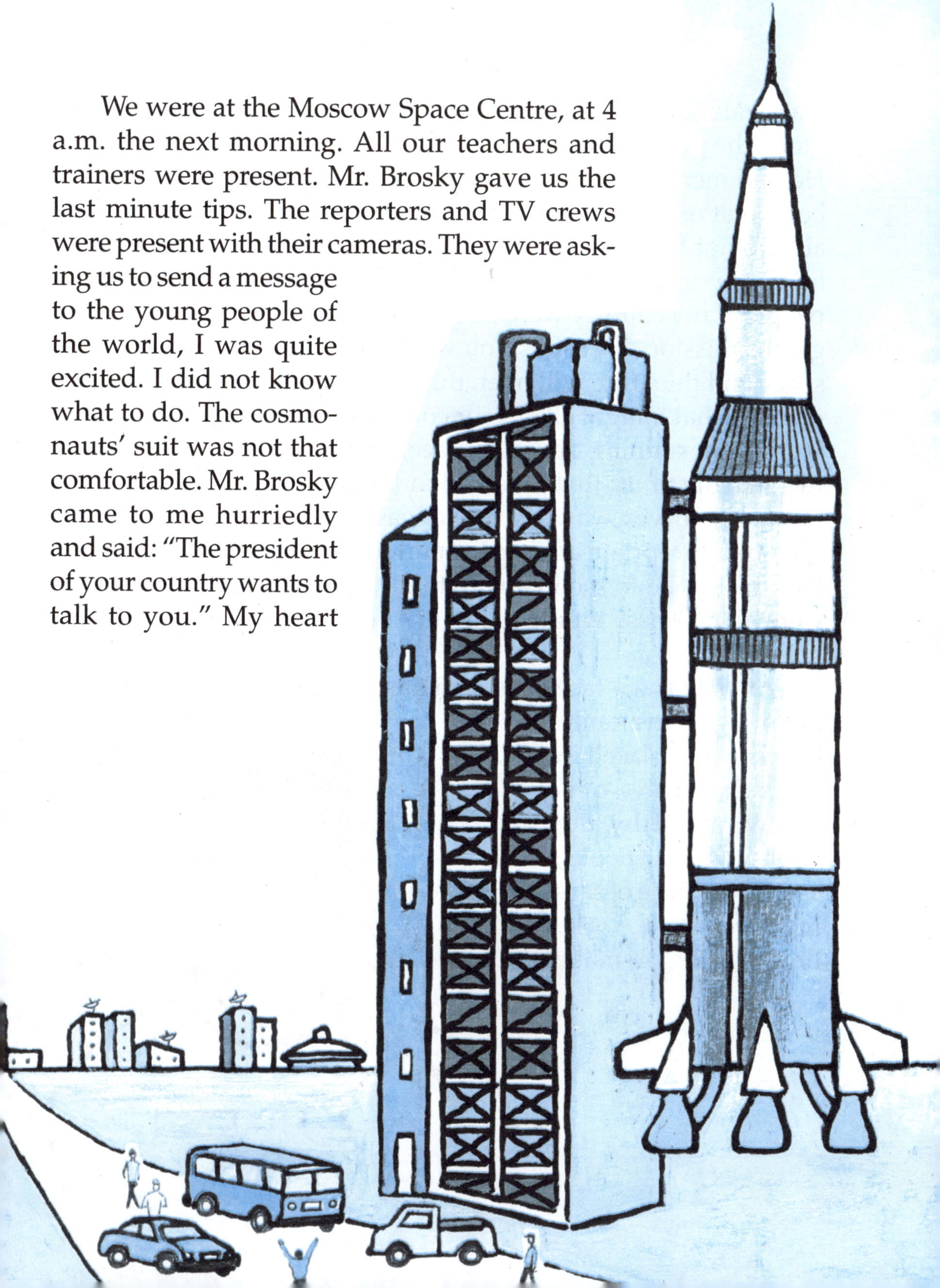

was beating fast, I liked him very much. My mouth was very dry. I took the phone, and said hello. His voice was kind and fatherly. He told me: "As you have shown until now, I hope that you will be a great researcher and an exemplary person with Islamic morals. Do not forget your responsibility towards your country and humanity in general." At the end he reassured me that all the people of my country were praying for me to succeed in this dangerous mission. He said: "You will be the first Iranian going into space and therefore will open this gate for your countrymen. Remember that tonight all of your compatriots are praying for you." Tears were running down my face, and my glasses became wet. Just like the times that I walked in the rain, I liked seeing things in a topsy-turvey way. My throat was so clogged that I could not give an appropriate answer to so much kindness. I only thanked him. He spoke to me in a way that my father would have, if he were alive. These words made my burden heavier. I wiped my glasses.

After that we faced the cameras and projectors again. They put our gear in a car to be taken and placed in the rocket. Three clergymen stood by the door with their books, as the last phase of saying goodbye. Mr. Brosky said: "To make

you feel better these three holy men will make you pass under the holy books. For Frederick, Matsu and Nooshka, the Bible, for Helmut, the Torah and for Abtin, the Quran."

Nooshka said: "Does the word of God differ?" Helmut said: "But they all belong to the one and only God and his words." I said: "All three will connect us to His unique presence, therefore all our holy to us."

All five of us passed under the three holy books and asked the Almighty for help. Even if Garshasp, my Zorostrian friend, had come too, we would all have passed under the Avesta as well. The Lord is the source of all religions, therefore all religions are holy.

With this we had shown the world the first step in friendship. Without us realising it, all the reporters and photographers clapped for us. Mr. Brosky rushed to us and kissed our foreheads. He said: "How beautifully you young people expressed and acted out that which the scholars of religion and science have said for thousands of years. How happy I am to have chosen you." The excitement of the trip was far more than us realising our important deed. We saw Victor. He was crying like a child and hugged each of us and kissed our hair. He was still anxious to come and cook for us. He did not know that we had to eat our paste from tubes like toothpaste. He was praying for us. We ran towards our special car. The strong wind, which was caused by the rocket's motors, was bothering us. When we were inside the car, everyone waved to us. The moment of bidding farewell is a sad moment. We did not know whether beyond the atmosphere we would still be alive or not. Maybe we would turn into a piece of coal and fall down, or float up in the skies beyond the atmosphere, outside of the earth's gravity. Goodbye, Earth! Farewell, you good people of the Earth! Will we see you again?

Suddenly, we were inside the Soyuz. The sky was still dark. From behind the windows we could see the lights on the other side where everyone had gathered to see the lift off. Each of us sat on our special chairs. We fastened our seatbelts. One of the employees came and fastened our head-gears to our suits, tightly, in a way that no air came in or out. The doctor had told us the manner of breathing correctly. The air and oxygen was flowing smoothly in our suits and head-gears. I felt my heart beating fast.

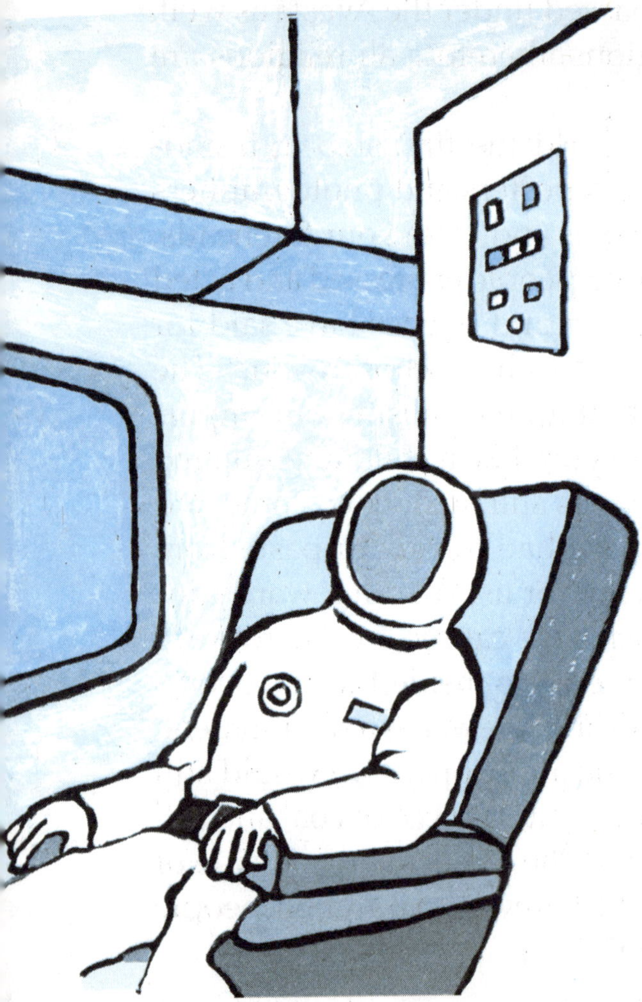

Mr. Veronick had taught us how to get energy and calm our anxiety and fright. Until now, the affair was like child's play for me. But this reality that I had accepted a great danger and risk made me think. I tried to remember my last conversation with my mother, my president and all the people who had taught me and loved me. The count down had started. I tried to remember God above all. When they announced the last number, I entrusted to God with my whole being. I shut my eyes for a second. I suddenly felt my guts being pulled down. I pressed my seat backwards and I lay flat on my back. I remembered Professor Krokansha's words. He said that the lowest

speed at first would be 40,000 kilometers an hour. They call this 'Running Speed'. At that moment the weight of our bodies would be ten times as much. The advantage of Soyuz was that it worked automatically. Our head-gear had only a small glass section in front. Therefore, I could not guess the position of my companions. But when I estimated Nooshka and Frederick's weight, I laughed with myself. I felt dizzy. My head ached and my eyes were burning. I felt something between a dream and reality, a strange and new feeling that I had never experienced before. A long time passed, I had lost track of time. A big jolt stopped us. I felt very scared. All of a sudden the ceiling opened up and two cosmonauts whom we had seen in Professor Krokansha's television came inside and pulled our numb bodies out through the ceiling. We passed through a large canal, and were placed somewhere. I still did not feel allright. The cosmonauts took off my head-gear and my suit. Helmut and Matsu were lying down somewhere and the cosmonauts were taking off the space suits of others. Soon, I fell asleep.

When I woke up, I realised that I was at a distance from the earth. My body was in a horizontal position and my head was lop-sided. Nooshka also looked funny with his blond hair and big tummy, especially when it went up and down. Matsu was sleeping with his glasses on, so that he could see his dreams better! And Frederick, with his wavy hair and black face, was snoring and his arms were hanging by his side. Then why was I an early riser? Maybe because I always rose early to pray. Waking them up was easy. It would have taken just a punch in their sides.

When everyone woke up, we laughed at our floating situation. Matsu said: "Did you notice kids, our heads hang lower than our bodies." One of the cosmonauts who had woken up to the sound of our conversation, came to the cabin where we were stationed. He had blond hair and blue eyes. He introduced himself as Sasha. Each of us shook hands with him and introduced ourselves. He was wearing a shirt and white trousers and he spoke softly so as not to wake his friend.

He said: "The first thing that will be surprising for you is that, here every 45 minutes is a day and night." Nooshka said joyfully, "Then we must constantly have lunch, supper and breakfast." Sasha looked at him and from his figure and big stomach realised that he must be greedy. He laughed and said: "No! Here is a large clock which is set to Moscow time, and we eat and sleep by this 'hour and time'." After that, as I was floating, I went to the window. For the first time I saw a view that I had never seen in my life. I saw an infinite blue space and below the horizon of our

sight, the earth. We would pass above it quickly, and we would rotate around it. The oceans, mountains, forests...Suddenly, I felt a strange love in my heart. I am attached to this large ball. This mother of all mothers... this protector of all things alive. Now, the fever of poetry that had subsided in me, was running in my veins, and that which flowed in my heart and mind poured out of my mouth.

*I say this for you, Earth,*
*our home our haven.*
*For your sprouts, creators,*
*living thing...*

And I ran towards my paper and pencil. I found a pen and piece of paper on the desk where the computer was placed, and wrote my poem. Quiet and silent, the kids were pressed to the window and flabbergastedly looked outside. It was strange, suddenly it was night and I was still writing. Nooshka called me: "Come, we can see the light of the cities from here." The situation was quite unusual. It was night quickly, then it would be day. Sasha asked us to follow him, to show us the different sections of the station, and have breakfast as well. The large clock showed 8 o'clock. Now it was 8 o'clock in Moscow. Floating, we followed him through a tube. He explained that the station had five sections, a dining room, two cabins for sleeping and a wagon for carrying trash. Each part of these sections was made of a thirteen-meter tube. In the main cabin, another cosmonaut was sitting behind a computer and was relaying news to earth. Sasha introduced us to Pavel. Pavel shook hands with us and we introduced ourselves. A well equipped computer was there. I had never seen anything like it. Matsu floated around the computer and kept expressing his joy and wonder at seeing it. Pavel who had turned his back towards us and was working on the computer, did not pay any attention to Matsu.

I said: "Professor Nicola had told us that the most complete antennas were set in the Mir Station." Sasha said: "The best freezers, a meticulous laboratory and an equipment for analyzing gases." Frederick said: "If a supermarket had been next to it, it would have been good, I would have invited everyone for chocolates." Everyone laughed. Even Pavel who seemed to be a glum person. Helmut asked: "Has it ever happened that no one was in the Mir Station?" Sasha said: "At least two people are to be present at the station all the time."

In another part of the main room, two other equipment were present. I asked: "What are these for?" Sasha said: "Exercise. Since we don't have enough movement here, they have put a stationary bicycle and tread-mill for us to exercise. We gathered together for breakfast. Each of us had a tube to put in our throats and press so that the food would go to our stomach. I thought of Victor and his breakfasts. I missed him. Matsu told Sasha: "Victor wanted to come here and cook for us." Sasha said: "I supposed he wanted to wash the pots and pans too." We were all laughing when Pavel came in. He took a tube from the fridge. He injected some water in it and started eating it. He was serious. Quietly, Helmut said: "Pavel reminds me of Mr. Volkof," and we laughed. Pavel did not like this joke. He gave us a sharp glance and said: "Is your schedule today lazing about?" Then he wrote a list of the things we had to do on a large white-board and said: "As an exception I give you time till 10 o'clock to look everywhere to satisfy your curiosity. After that you must follow your daily programme. Your schedule includes sports, working on the computer, relaying information, working in the lab, writing the report of what you've worked on and transmitting it to earth. Each of you can speak with your family for five minutes. Eating breakfast, lunch and supper... reading, listening to music, watching television, etc. in your free time. By the way, I hate useless chattering."

We all looked at him in disbelief. We did not expect someone to treat us like this way up in the sky. Nooshka asked: "Are there computers and laboratories for each of us or do we have to work on them one by one?" Pavel shook his head and said: "No, therefore we all have to take turns in working and exercising." Nooshka suggested: "Then it is better to write the work hours on the white board as well. In that case everyone would know his duties precisely." Pavel wrote our names plus his own and Sasha's and specified our work hours. Each of us had two hours of computers, one hour of exercise and two hours of lab work.

We had until twelve o'clock to look around the station, therefore we floated towards the rooms. I said: "Isn't it strange that our heads are down and our legs are high up?" Helmut said: "It's because of our brains." Matsu said: "What brain do you have, you lowly bookworm?" Pavel yelled from the other side: "Be

polite to each other." But we took no notice.

Frederick said: "But when my head is down and my legs are up, I don't feel secure." Helmut said: "Although there is no gravity, one knows that this is a strange situation, meaning we're

upside down." Floating we went to the rooms and once again we had a good look. I was enjoying myself. The ceiling of all the cabins were white, the walls light blue and the floors brown, orange and green.

We went to the windows again, to see the lakes, mountains and rivers...

I thought of my mother and my sister who should be at school right now. They could not see me in the sky, because our ship was very small and very fast. Soon it was night and we watched the lights of the cities. In each of these houses life goes on. I asked myself: "Did you ever think you'd see the earth from this distance?" Sasha put his hand on my shoulder and said: "Your expression is very poetical." I said: "Well, sometimes I write poetry." Sasha laughed. It was daylight. He pointed to the earth.

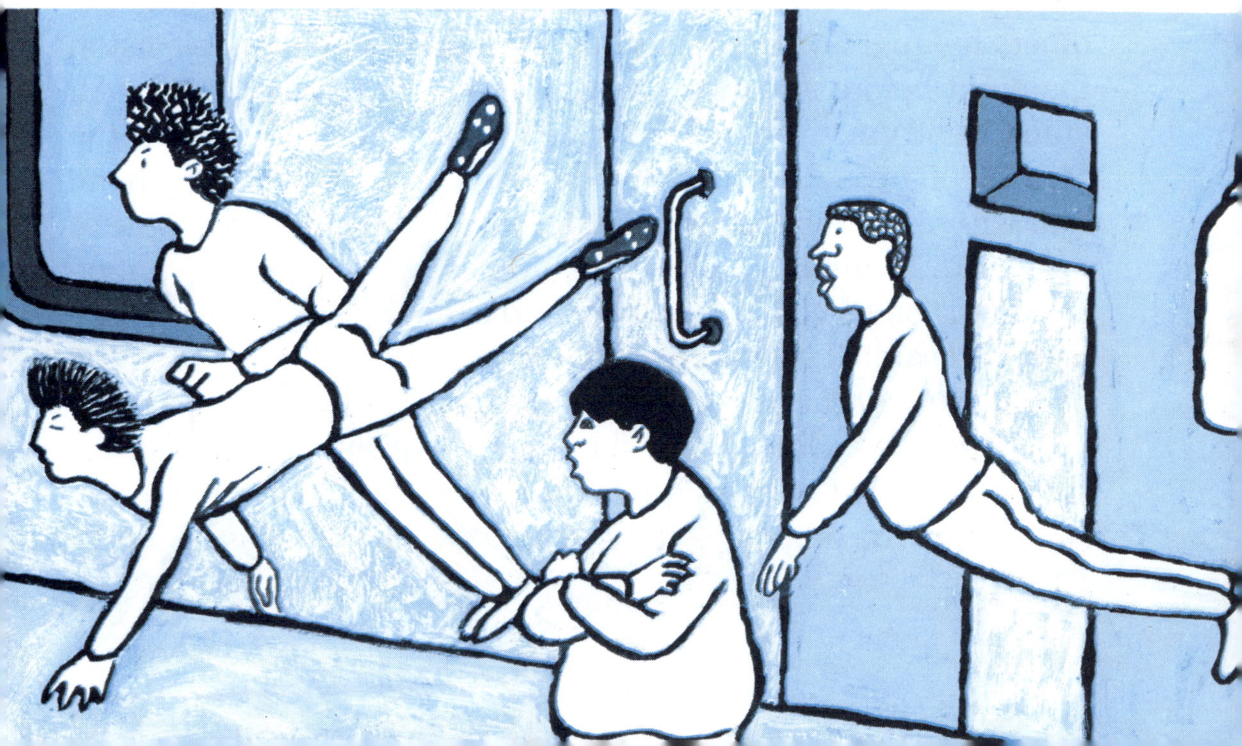

"That part is Iran." My heart trembled. And I said loudly: "Iran? Iran?" Sasha said: "Iranovich. Do you know what it means?" I said: "No!" He said: "It means Paradise." At this time my compatriots were having a nice day. They were working or trying to learn. What were they after? Oh, Iran, Iranovich. Sasha said: "Exactly at twelve o'clock we'll have a beautiful sight." Pavel yelled: "Mr. Brosky wants to talk to the kids." We all rushed towards where Pavel was sitting. He transmitted our picture through the television screen to Mr. Brosky. And we saw Mr. Brosky on television. We loved him with his blue eyes and missed him. He asked us to gather together so that he could see the faces of all of us. We all laughed and waved to him. He said: "Pavel's planning is good, please don't waste time. Don't forget what you told me about humanity, life and construction."

It was over. I felt good. My feeling of estrangement and being alone in space had subsided. My mother was on the phone. I was happy to hear her voice.

As long as I remember, she has always been my source of energy. While I was talking I had floated up, and this made the others to laugh. Mother said that she had seen me on television the night before and that she was proud of me. She said: "All your countrymen prayed for you so that you would reach the Mir Station in one piece. Remember that you are indebted to them. This trip was provided for you by each of them and the people of the world. Therefore, don't waste time." My sister took the phone and said: "Since you are up there and cannot tease me, I am very happy." I said: "I intend to send a shooting star to your room." I had hardly put the phone down that Matsu's mother called.

At twelve o'clock, I saw the most beautiful view I had ever seen in my life. On one side the moon and the stars were in the sky, and on the other side the sun and the earth. It was beyond

my belief. For the duration that our eyes held this amazing sight on the horizon, there was silence.

Day and night kept coming and going, without any pause.

After lunch, everyone went about his work, as scheduled. After half an hour of rest, it was time for my exercise. I cycled on the stationary bicycle for a while, and then I ran on the treadmill. Exercising made me feel fresh. It was time for ten minutes of rest and then what they had left for me to work on, in the lab. It was a biological test which I had to carry out and I had to record the result. I had an hour of relaxation after that. Then I studied the research I had carried out on earth, and which was recorded on a diskette and placed at my disposal, once again. In this situation I had to review my work, so that if I had made any mistakes or if there were any problems I could correct them myself. The five minutes of conversation with my mother had taken the fatigue out of my body. At the moment of parting, she had given me a book in English and had asked me to read it in my free time. Now, she had asked me if I had read it, but I almost had no free time nor was I likely to have any.

Sasha said: "Children, it's time for supper." So we all went to the dining cabin. We put the tubes in our mouths, it did not taste bad, but since it was unusual, it did not give a feeling of satisfaction. Then we each went to a corner to catch some sleep, in a floating position. But every forty-five minutes night would turn into day and vice-versa. When it would become daylight, sleep would vanish from my eyes and I would become frustrated. Sasha brought us five blinders (eye-shutters). Then he exclaimed: "Look at him!" Helmut had opened a book and covered his face with it. I said: "That is not strange, because he is a bookworm." Frederick was sleeping without any shutters and he was snoring. Therefore, three blinders were enough. I felt Sasha wanted to ask why

Helmut is a bookworm, but since we were tired, he went to his own cabin.

The alarm clock rang, it was exactly 8 o'clock in the morning. When we had gathered around, Sasha said: "Helmut, last night the kids were saying you're a bookworm." He took out his breakfast tube and laughed and said: "What are they, themselves? This big one is a black cow. That one is a bat. This is a cobra, and that one obviously is a bear." Sasha's cheeks became red from laughter. Pavel laughed a little but tried to contain himself. He looked at Sasha and said: "You see, I guessed correctly. They have hardly arrived and they have started fighting. What funny names they've given each other. They have come here to learn the new technology to be able to disintegrate and kill each other better." We were all silent. The meaning of Pavel's words did not sink in our minds. Why should we fight. Nooshka raised his arm and said: "Excuse me. Who wants to fight?" Pavel was angry. He said: "You!" And he pointed to all of us. Nooshka said: "But we love each other very much. Why should we fight." Sasha got up from his chair, and we followed him. As planned, it was time to work. Two of us started the analysis which had to be done in the lab. Two others started studying the given plans on the computer, and one worked out on the bicycle. All of us were hurt by Pavel's words. From the beginning of our trip no one, not even Mr. Volkof who seemed high-strung, had ever talked of war and fighting.

When it was my turn in the laboratory, they put some protein at my disposal to study. Lab work was always attractive to me, because I would find a lead and would go on. I would witness certain activities and would write down my observations. When I finished my work I usually had a good feeling, like finding the answer to a puzzle. I had to follow up my fact-finding research which had some shortcomings in the early phase, on this computer. Mr. Brosky had jotted down some of my mistakes.

I had given a plan for fact-finding and he had pointed out its shortcomings. He had written a note for me: "Work on it, I hope you can succeed."

Whenever my eyes became tired I would go the window, and watch the colourful globe of the Earth. There were so many stars in the sky that I wondered at my smallness and the vastness of the galaxies.

Sasha kindly came to my side and asked: "When you look at the earth, what do you feel?" I said: "I miss it. I appreciate it very much. Whenever I look at the stars, I feel tiny. Much more than I felt on the earth."

Sasha said: "In comparison to this universe, our life is very insignificant. Apart from our smallness and our diminutiveness, the span of our life is short. Here, it is a question of millions of years."

I said: "Your words remind me of a story my mother had told me of butterflies which are born in the morning and die at night. My mother would say despite the shortness of their life, flowers are their companions, and since they add to the beauty of nature, we can say they have a useful existense."

Sasha laughed and went deep in thought. I knew he was thinking of his past. Had his life been like a butterfly? What about my future? Will I live like a butterfly?

Typing was always the last part of our assignment. Because Mr. Brosky was unhappy with the handwriting of some of us, therefore he deemed it necessary for us to type the result of our research. At seven o'clock our work was almost finished. We could have some free time. The programmes on television were not interesting, so we gathered around and talked of our past memories. Then we practiced the melody of the song that we were supposed to compose. The tune was not pleasant in many places. So, for the second time Frederick had to rewrite it. Fortunately, the computers were programmed for music as well. Thus we fed the notes into the computer. It was time for the words. I read the poem I had written.

*We write this for you, oh, Earth*
*Our Station and our refuge for the world*
*that blossoms in your womb, you*
*Symbol of kindness*
*Remain for us*
*We are together, singular and unique*
*By the window that opens into heaven*
*In a night that tells us of a great secret, we look at you*
*Remain for us.*

They all clapped for me. Matsu said: "It's nice but it's short." Frederick said: "We five are unique, does it include that?" I said: "No, all people are individuals. All are unique, like their finger prints!"

Helmut said: "Go and stand by the window again, maybe you will feel like writing poetry again." I said: "First see if you can put music to this much or not? I will read the rest of it to you in good time."

It was time to call our families. One by one we went to the phone and talked to our families for five minutes each.

When my mother heard that I had written a poem, she became happy. She asked me: "Have you read the book I gave you?" Ashamed, I said: "No." My sister said: "Many people have called and asked how you are. They have prayed for you and wished you well. I have written their names, so that when you come back, god-willing, I can give them to you."

The knowledge that I was remembered by friends and others paid attention to me, made me happy.

Pavel still rarely met with us. He tried to do his own work, he was not happy to see us and ate alone.

When it was time to sleep, each of us took eye-shaders, but Helmut preferred a book. And Frederick, jokingly said: "My eyelids are so black that I do not need any shades."

At mid-night I woke up with a headache and a feeling of vomiting. I could not open my eyes from the pain in my head. In that bad situation, somebody moved me quickly. The sound of air-conditioning echoed in my ears. A hand slapped me, softly. I opened my eyes, it was Pavel.

He gave me a pill along with a tube which contained water. When I took the pill, Pavel said: "I woke up to the sound of your moaning." Then he caressed my hair, gently. May be he was a

kind man after all. The sound of my groaning had woken him up. Quietly, he continued: "Whenever you want to sleep, put your head next to the ventilator. Since there is no gravity here, warm air does not go up, like on earth, it stays where it is. When you are asleep, a large carbon dioxide bubble surrounds your head. Now, little by little, you'll feel better."

He stayed beside me until I fell asleep. When I woke up in the morning, I felt well. Pavel told everyone about the previous night. At breakfast Sasha explained to everyone to remember to sleep beside the ventilator fans. Helmut said: "Abtin nearly died." Then they all started to joke around. Floating, I lay flat, as though I was dead. Work started again. When I was carrying on my research on the computer, Pavel sat beside me. I told him about the training that we had had. And I told him that I had proposed an information out-put system for everyone, on a large scale, but I was not able to complete it. Mr. Brosky had some positive criticism, and that I was studying it again. Pavel looked at me for a while and asked: "What would you like to inform the people of the world of?"

I said: "I want to invent a method in which everyone can find out everything in all countries, with the least expense."

Pavel asked: "Suppose this invention is complete and you are able to connect the whole world with a cheap and simple communication network, what is the first thing you have to say to people as an inventor?" I said: "Love, peace, constructiveness."

Pavel said: "For thousands of years, men and women have said these things, but when they have come to power, all their promises have become the opposite in their deeds."

I said: "Maybe among them there existed some honest people, but their voices were not loud enough, or their communication was limited. When one thinks of positive things, he becomes constructive and responsible."

Pavel went deep into thought. Then he got up from my side and went to the window and started looking at the earth and the stars.

Frederick said: "It's twelve o'clock." Hearing this, we all went running to the window. What a beautiful sight! How can I put this view into words? Frederick said: "Abtin, hurry up and compose a poem." Pavel said: "This beautiful ball in which our world becomes a reality is 4600 million years old. How many hearts do you think are beating there? How many plants live on it? Life is life, an ant, a pigeon or a human."

"This earthly globe is constantly changing, it is getting old. Its old age is premature. We have not taken care of our mother well. We are on it, we are fed, we breathe, we endeavour and work, but we are not responsible enough to safe-guard it. It is coughing and it has fever."

We all laughed, we thought Pavel was joking. Matsu said: "Coughing? Is it a man?"

Pavel said: "Yes, its volcanoes have become active, and all the time they are spewing their lava. Its surface has become hot, it has a fever. Its cover, which was made of trees and plants has fallen off, or I had better say, humans have felled its trees." Helmut said: "Meaning it has become bald?"

Pavel took no notice of our laughter. "Its breathing system has become disordered. The oxygen gas which should be given to our lungs is not enough. The layer that it should form to protect us like a sheet, from the sun and its harmful rays, has been torn." Matsu opened and closed his small eyes several times and said: "Sheet? Does it want to sleep?" Pavel asked Matsu: "What do you know about the atmosphere?" Matsu said: "That..." Sasha asked us: "Do you know about the greenhouse phenomenon?"

Matsu said; "This is a case that I am researching. When we go up, the atmosphere exists to the height of eight-hundred kilometers, in which of course the higher layers are thin.

The atmosphere is in reality the lining of the earth. It is made of a kind of oxygen gas, which contains three atoms, called ozone. Acting as a filter, this gas avoids the penetration of some harmful rays of the sun." Sasha asked us about the other function of the atmosphere. I said: "This relates to my research. The other function of atmosphere is the reflection of some radio waves on a large scale. This means that it actually spreads radio waves." Sasha said: "Then, Matsu, you do accept that the atmosphere is a sheet or lining for covering the earth. Yes?" Matsu laughed and said: "Yes, I was just joking." Pavel said: "This disorder in the atmospheric situation has caused a 'green-house phenomenon' that means an up-side down climate. The contaminated gases remain on the surface of the earth and we have to breathe them. Toxic gases which slowly poison the living creatures, devastate the plants, make water creatures extinct and cause strong storms."

Night fell. From up there the cities were distinct with their lights on. Sasha said: "In those houses, there are children who have started life happily and full of hope. But our predecessors, even us, what have we left for them?"

Quite seriously Nooshka said: "A planet earth, old, bald with the flu, covered with a sheet with holes in it."

The sound of our laughter was so loud, that if there had been neighbours next to the Mir Station, they would have told us off. Sasha admitted that it had been a long time that he had not laughed like that.

Pavel said: "O.K. kids, lets look at it, seriously. Why has this earth, which is our point of reliance and dependence, become like this?"

I said: "Because of the careless use of chemical goods, weapons and emptying the forests of trees." Sasha said: "Yes, our predecessors have poisoned the environment, and worst of all is radioactive material." Matsu punched Frederick on the side, and said: "Do you understand! They mean Hiroshima and Nakazaki." Pavel said: "Matsu, let's suppose that you have grown up and become a scientist, knowledgeable in making fatal equipment, who will you get your revenge from, for Hiroshima?" Matsu looked at all of us hesitantly and said: "I shall not become a scientist to become active in the technique of destroying people. I don't intend to get vengeance from anyone."

Pavel asked: "Then who should revenge these poor people?" Matsu said: "I've come to try another experiment. I want to construct, not destruct." Pavel asked: "Is that right? Then why have you named your friends bear, cow, snake and worm?" Matsu said: "Because I am a bat myself."

We laughed loudly, again.

Pavel said: "Then, you're not a true friend."

Matsu said: "Why yes, I am a true friend."

Pavel said: "Helmut! Hitler burned many of your forefathers in the ovens."

Helmut said: "He was uncouth. He had not gone to kindergarten."

Pavel said: "Everything cannot be a joke. Who will you get your forefathers' revenge from?"

Helmut said: "No one. I've come to find a solution, to forget the ugly memories of the past. I want to convince all the people of my age that the past is past, and it has nothing to do with our present and future. We have only come to serenade love and friendship."

Pavel faced Frederick. It was day time again. He said jokingly:

"While it is light and you're not lost in darkness, tell me, how do you find white people?" Frederick said: "Empty-headed creatures, like myself, but white."

Sasha cut our laughter short with a gesture of his hand, and asked: "Don't you want to settle your account with those who call you nigger?"

Frederick said: "No! Because they themselves are white-niggers. I've only come to take the message of peace for black people. We are all human, and we must live side by side on this sick planet. We all share one thing: earth, water, air and food."

Pavel asked: "Nooshka, what will you do?" Nooshka answered: "I'm a bear without any danger. I like fish and honey... and most of all, life. I've decided to forget the wars that have bloodied the soil of my country, and to give all the children of my age a machine for forgetting. I don't like to keep the rust of bad memories and war and revenge in my heart. I want to build a new world."

Sasha said: "Abtin, because of your Islamic ideology, you crave war, you suppressed your neighbour although he was a Moslem."

I said: "I have not become a war-monger. I'm a Moslem and a Moslem means a person wanting well-being and peace. I detest these wars. I have seen and felt war with my nerves, blood and flesh. I hate war from the bottom of my heart. When I was only two-years of age, a man from a neighbouring country, who apparently was responsible for leading the country, got an idea in his head to conquer my land. His country is vast, it is fertile. It has plenty of oil, and in proportion to its population it occupies a large area of land on our planet Earth.

"He attacked my country without any warning. At a time that everyone was coming home, unaware, from a hard-day's work, when they were faced with an unwanted war. The enemy was armed, ready for war, whereas the people of my country were defenseless. Even so, they fought a manly war.

"For eight years, it was war and bloodshed, for nothing... like all other men, my father went to face the enemy, to protect our land, and he was killed."

For my condolence, a sad silence prevailed. Night had fallen, and I could see many stars in the galaxy.

I continued: "Thus, my father was satisfied for a stupid self-indulgence. That foolish and blind man, had to be satisfied with his own land, after killing so many people. A satisfaction that he later proved false."

Pavel asked: "Don't you want to revenge your father's blood?"

I respond: "That I should rob many of fatherly love, like myself? No, never! I, like my friends, am struggling for peace, love and constructiveness. The sound heard from my soul is only the song of love." Pavel was silent for a while. Then he bent his head and said: "I owe an apology to all of you, I misjudged you."

Sasha and Pavel were excited. Dawn had come and it was daytime, again. All of us were looking at the old Earth. Our glances were loving, for it and all its creatures.

It was time for lunch. We gathered together. This time Pavel was with us too.

# 7

Pavel said: "I have seen some mistakes in your calculations which you have recorded in your computers. I shall discuss them with each of you, in the afternoon. My experience rejects some of the suggestions you have made in connection with your proposed plans, which I shall explain to you, too. I hope you reach a result soon."

He made all of us happy. I said: "Without a guide we would have to make many mistakes to become experienced." Sasha said: "Experiment and failure is good for research, but it needs a large amount of time."

The atmosphere had become more friendly and we were all benefitting from it. When there is peace, security comes with it. When there is security, the mind is free. One can think, work and become less tired. I went to the lab again which was situated at a corner of the small room, and started analysing the particular protein. Nooshka had gone on the treadmill and was running. His leaps made the station move. Just like sitting on a motor-boat when another boat passes by it. I raised my head and protested. Pavel came to my side. Annoyed, I said: "This big bear does not let me finish my experiment. The movements cause the material to crystallize." By putting a lever under the microscope, he made a special magnetic field that made the microscope's plate to remain stationary. I was astonished, because it prevented my protein from becoming crystallized. I asked Pavel: "Who invented this?"

Pavel said: "Somebody like you, who cared about the betterment of situation in life."

Pavel left my side. I called him back. He looked at me and slowly sat down next to me. I said: "I w ant to make a confession. At first I thought of this trip lightly. I thought it was impossible. Then I was scared and then I felt insecure. But now, I think I have entered a special world that I could never imagine. You know, everything seems bigger than my thoughts, mind and power. But as more time passes, I have more access to them. A feeling of being valuable. I never imagined I would be able to see the planet Earth from up here. To experiment with iron and protein. To give information through computers, and understand the complicated space systems."

Pavel said: "Don't forget what I told you."

I said: "About what?"

He said: "About the Earth becoming old and ugly. If you can find a solution for that, then you're a man."

Sasha was behind the television set. Joyfully he yelled: "Tomorrow a 'progress' will arrive. I hope we'll have lots of clothes, packages and letters. These kids have used all our water savings."

We were all astonished. Sasha explained that 'progress' is a small wagon, which when it reaches us, brings clean clothes, food, fuel, water and necessary equipment for repairing the Station.

Nooshka asked: "It means that an astronaut flies it here and then returns?" Sasha said: "Progress' is without a pilot and it automatically attaches itself to the Station." I asked: "How do they control it?"

Sasha said: "All the activities are controlled by radio from Moscow. After 'Progress' arrives, we empty its contents and fill it with dirty clothes, and all the unusable stuff from the garbage containers and toilets."

Nooshka asked: "Then all these are taken back to the center in Moscow?"

Sasha said: "No. After entering the Earth's atmosphere, they are destroyed."

Frederick said: "I hope Mr. Volkof has sent us some chocolates."

It was 8 o'clock in the evening. We didn't have much work left. I was tired, but happy because I had learned, and experienced a lot.

We gathered to eat dinner. Tonight, we had shrimp with vegetables that were in a tube as paste. Frederick tasted a bit and said: "It's delicious, but since it is in paste form, it's unusual for me." Nooshka said: "Think of Victor, if he were here he would make us some chicken dish."

I said: "But this tastes good, too."

Helmut asked me. "Have you finally read the book your mother told you to read or not?"

I burst out laughing, since Helmut opens that book, and puts it on his face. I said: "I'm waiting for you to finish it first, and then give it to me." Helmut said: "But when I read that book, my eyes are closed."

The children laughed.

Pavel asked: "What is the name of the book?"

Floating, Helmut went to the bedroom and brought it. The title was 'Resistance' and its author was Alfred Lancing.

Sasha said: "I've read this book. It's about discovering the South Pole." I said: "Is it possible for you to tell me a little about it?" Sasha said: "In comparison to what these discoverers have borne, this space station is like a five-star hotel. They had to eat the meat of sea lions and penguins for days on end, while we have the best food." He raised his tube and said: "Shrimp, borsch, vegetables... and you know what else... Now they're in a paste form." Nooshka said: "All the better, because we don't have to chew it."

Sasha continued: "They've spent one winter in darkness, whereas we have day and night every forty-five minutes. They watched endless white on the ground, but we can see all the beauty of the Himalayas and the Italian boot and the Cape of Good Hope, and enjoy it. They did not change their clothes for one year, whereas, here, we wear a fresh set of clothes every week. They had to cross the highs and lows of the uneven terrain, whereas for us it's this poor station that moves and takes us around. The heat here is controlled and we have light for brightness. We have computers, television, telephone and god knows how many blessings. But they had none of these."

Pavel said: "So you're saying that we have a kingly life!"

We all laughed, and I realised why my mother had bought me this book, and insisted on my reading it.

Early the next morning, we woke up to a jolt. Sasha and Pavel went to the garage, which had space for three space crafts (Soyuz).

'Progress' had arrived. All of us were happy and smiling and gathered around it. There were seven sets of underclothes and clothes with our names written on each. Water and necessary material for the Station, food and a number of tubes containing chocolate, with this message written on them: "Mr. Brosky's gift for the young scholars." Letters and pictures for Pavel and Sasha. Happier than anyone were Frederick and Nooshka. They jumped up and down and the station moved with their movement.

Soon we went to the cabins and put on our clean clothes. We all helped to put the garbage and sewage into the 'Progress'. With

the help of some levers, Sasha separated it from the Station. 'Progress' distanced itself from us to go aflame in the earth's atmosphere and disintegrate.

The day ended happily. After eating breakfast, each of us had a tube of chocolate.

Frederick said: "Helmut, you won't eat all of your chocolate, put the rest of it in the fridge." Helmut put his tongue out and said: "So that like the last time you can eat it?"

Nooshka said: "You don't like it, so at least let us eat it."

Helmut said: "I like it very much." And he put the tube in his shirt's pocket. I wanted to see the 'Progress' bursting into flames. For this, I floated to the window. The cream-coloured, dusty clouds over the African desert were expanding. I had seen this scenery many many times. I said: "Pavel, why are the clouds over the African desert cream-coloured?"

Pavel came to the window. The children came next to me, one by one, and we watched the outside view.

Pavel said: "About time! It's good that you have talked about that."

"I wanted to tell you about the illness of the planet Earth. But I felt talking about it saddens me. But, now pay close attention: See that the colour of the oceans is not blue but gray. Sand storms rise from the beaches and the large deserts of Africa. Look at that lake. Once upon a time it was large, but now only a crooked spot is left. This is the Amazon jungle that's burning, do you see its smoke? These trees that are perishing in the fire are the producers of oxygen on earth. People cut the trees and make farms out of the land. The plants die and their empty place is like a core on the ground.

"The Tennessee Yoga River flows down from the Central Madagascar mountains, with lots of mud, while the jungles

around it disappear, and the hills are washed up on its route. The sky above the cities is hazy, a black smog is hanging between us and them." After that he looked into our eyes. There was a lot of sadness in his eyes. He was a scholar worried about the Earth and its environment. He showed us everything. He asked us: "What have you thought about for this endangered planet? How useful can you be for it?" We were brushing our teeth and getting ready for bed, one by one, when the power was cut. I had experienced a power cut many times before, but there the situation was different. At those times I was on the ground and now I was in space, void of the earth's gravity. I trembled with fright. Absolute darkness. This belongs to another world. With a shaky voice, Helmut yelled from the cabin: "Why have the lights gone off?" Sasha said: "We have a power cut." Until that moment I had not realised that the sound of the ventilators and engines were humming in my ears, since I had gotten used to it. But now there was silence, absolute silence. For one second I asked myself: "Have I gone deaf?" Frederick said: "Without the ventilators we have no air and soon we'll suffocate." Pavel's voice could be heard from afar and he was comforting us.

I said: "You yourself said that warm air does not go up." Pavel said, calmly: "What do you mean up? Here the Earth's laws do not apply."

Nooshaka said: "Well, when there is no movement of air, without the fans, anhydride carbonic gas will form a bubble around our heads and we shall die."

At this point, Sasha and Pavel went towards the electric canals with very powerful flashlights. The five of us were staying huddled up.

Matsu said: "As it was, I didn't feel secure, let alone now that we don't even have electricity."

We were all anxious and frightened. After a while, suddenly there was light everywhere, and the humming sound of the ventilators could be heard. Our faces were amusing. Worry had made our faces funny. We hugged each other out of delight and cheered. Like two heroes, Sasha and Pavel came to our side. Pavel said: "If one day the planet Earth becomes threatened, what will the people of the world do?"

"If five young people raise their voices which is the echo of the voices of thousands and thousands of youths for peace, development and love, it will be like what I did just now with this old and decrepit Station.'

*I write for you, oh Earth*
*You, our station and our refuge*
*For the world that blossoms in your womb,*
*you symbol of kindness*
*Remain for us*
*We are together, singular and unique*
*By the window that opens unto heaven*
*And in a night that tells us of a great secret*
*Remain for us*
*We are not afraid of the devils and their machine guns*
*We are not afraid of the tanks*
*that plow death and mines*
*that plant decadence and destruction*
*We shall make you flourish*
*Remain for us*
*We shall demolish the walls of separation and*
*build the bridges of love and kindness*
*Time will be ours*
*Remain for us*
*The stars are not that far from us*

*Look in our eyes*
*You will find a light full of hope*
*And we shall make you flourish again*
*And we shall invite the angels to the feast of love*
*Remain for us.*

## 8

Sasha said: "Mr. Brosky's on the television screen and he wants to see you."

From behind computers, microscopes and exercise machines, all of us rushed towards the television set. It was he himself. With his usual smile he gestured for us to stick together so that he could see us all. He called roll: "Rattle Snake?" I said: "Present." "Bat, Polar Bear?" "Present." "Black Cow?" "Present." "Earth-worm?" Helmut shook his head. "Bookworm, Sir!" Mr. Brosky laughed heartily and apologised. "Yes, yes, bookworm." "Present." "Well, kids, is life O.K. with you?" All of us said loudly, "Yes!" He said: "There is no doubt in that time is favourable to children. It has always been so. Today, it is exactly one month that you are in the Station. Next week a Soyuz will come to bring you back, and two other people will take the place of Pavel and Sasha. Consequently, add up all you've done. During this time you have travelled 12,000,000 kilometers." We did not let him finish his words. We mumbled and talked so much together that Mr. Brosky protestingly said: "Children, the cost of this conversation between you and I is very high. So listen to me, then say whatever you want to say. The song you sent me is very beautiful. I gave it to the directors of the symphonic orchestra whose music you went

to listen to the first day, to set it to music. I shall speak to you again. See you soon."

It was twelve o'clock, and at this hour our date was to stand at the window to watch the Earth and the sky. I don't know what it takes to watch this view. It is so beautiful that I am not able to portray it. Then I saw large hazy clouds on the African desert. Chad Lake is drying up. Five minutes later the Nile river and its banks, like the Sinai, the Red Sea and the rest are in front of our eye altogether, then the Caucasus Mountains, after that the Alborz Mountains covered with snow. Sasha said: "Abtin do you see the Alborz range?" I said: "This is the white-gowned bride of Iran." As we were standing by the window, watching the view, I related a story which I had read last year from 'The Stories of the Prophets'.

"When Zolgarnein[1] reached the Qaff (Alborz) Mountain, he saw that the mountain was surrounded by small mountains. He said to the mountains: Who are you? It said: Qaaf mountain. He said: Tell me what are these mountains surrounding you? The mountain replied: They are my veins. Whenever He wants to create an earthquake, He orders me and I shake one of my veins and in the lands attached to it an earthquake takes place.

Then in accordance to plea of Zolgarnein, Qaaf portrayed the greatness of God a little and added: Behind me there is a land which has been covered with snow and ice for the past five hundred years. If these mountains of snow and ice did not exist, the world would burn in heat as in hell." The kids laughed and I continued: "The Qaaf or Alborz Mountain is the nest of Simorq, which is one of the mythical figures in the stories of 'Shahnameh' by Ferdowsi, one of the poets of my country."[2]

*We possess a king of Right*
*Who is in pursuit of the Qaaf Mount*

*His name is Simorq, king of the birds*
*He, close to us but we quite afar*

Matsu said; "Tell us the rest of it too!" But I couldn't remember the rest of the Shahnameh. I promised to send each of them a Shahnameh translated into English, when we returned to Earth.

That night, I put my head next to the ventilator to sleep, but I couldn't sleep. I had traveled to a far away past. I remembered my childhood, my games, my classmates, my mother and the rest of the family. I remembered Mr. Brosky's words, I had traveled 12,000,000 kilometers in one month while my friends in Iran had gone to school and back. How time flies on a trip. I asked my heart: What period do you like the best for me to register in my mind? My childhood, earning first place in Olympiad? Being chosen for the trip to Moscow? Meeting the great space scholars of the world? Speaking with the President? Travelling to the Mir Station? Finding good friends?

My heart beat fast for all these achievements and moments, and I thanked the Almighty for all these blessings. I must try and sleep. We shall not be here more than another week, and I must accumulate all my research. I shall miss the Mir Station. The next morning we woke up earlier than usual. The more we neared the time of our return, the more we appreciated each other and the Mir Station. We sang our song loudly, together. Happily and fresh, we went to the dining cabin. Sasha said: "It's a pity, my research on fresh wheat has given a positive response. I would have liked to remain here until the last stage."

Pavel said: "A station which fifteen countries have invented will soon be put in the Earth's orbit, and this old Mir Station will be dismantled. How sad it is."

I said: "With the help of my peers, I wish to put an Iranian

Station in the orbit! The Station of love and friendship." Sasha said: "Constantly you speak of love. What is love in your opinion, actually?" Matsu said: "I believe that a better human being for his growth and development, must be bound by three elements: love, belief, knowledge. Love in my opinion is the relationship between the people of the Earth." Nooshka said: "Love and kindness is very valuable. It's worthy and pure, and since it is expensive, it's a long time before its counterfeit has been made too. Naturally, I have the authentic version. This can be seen inside us." Frederick said: "A good human being can experience love. A charitable person can be a source of good in a tribe."

Helmut said: "Love first appeared in a family. Then in neighbours and relatives, then in classmates and friends. Thus its circle expanded, until it became like mine which is as big as the Earth's globe."

We all whistled for him, for his big heart.

I said: "One day a philosopher thus said of love: God said: you, Man, I love you. When I created you, I had cleaned the earth before. When you were supposed to be born, I made your mother fall in love with you, so that she would feed you from the nectar of her beings, and guard you. At times her love is so strong that she forgets herself. I have created all the world, and beings for you, because I love you. But I have created you for myself."

Sasha said: "Therefore, God has fused his love for humans with action, and he proved it to us. But usually we only talk. What have we done for Him, truly, to tell Him we love him and we worship Him?"

We all fell silent... then love is not only sound, it is action as well.

When each of us went back to our work and experiments, I

felt this conversation left a special effect on me, and opened a new porthole of fresh thought for me.

Suddenly, Pavel yelled: "Kids come here by the television set. The international press want to have a programme with you as a last interview." Quickly, we went next to the television set. We could see their picture. Our faces were almost attached to each other, so that they could see all of us at once.

A reporter said: "I hope this trip will be full of good news for all of us. Recently, a few flying sorceress have been seen in the Earth's atmosphere, and sounds have been recorded conveying that some beings live in planets beyond our Earth. Do you have solutions to fight these beings?" We remained silent. It was a strange question. At this time another reporter asked: "How much chance do you think we have to confront space beings?"

All of a sudden Frederick jumped like a sparkle and with a voice that we could never have imagined shouted: "Enough, destruction is enough. Ethnic killing, Indian killing, Black killing, weak killing, how long should it last? How long do you want to destruct so that you have a better share? The first toy you gave us was a gun. For the next game, you taught us how to use it. To kill. To destroy. Later when we grew older, you gave us the real thing to exterminate people with. You said: 'For the love of humanity, kill humans, with war planes. Mortars, bombs, missiles…' for what?"

Matsu, whose glasses had slipped down on his nose, straightened his glasses and yelled: "The first cartoons of my life were full of wars between humans and space beings and robots which mixed our innocent and clean minds with war."

The reporters seemed pale and looked at us with surprise. One said: "It seems you are not as comfortable as you should be up there, because you've become aggressive." I said: "On the contrary, we were quite comfortable being away from you selfish warmongers, for a while. Why aren't you concerned about life with peace? Why didn't you ask us about the well-being of the Earth?"

"Until when must you bring up the children of the world like fighting cocks, to turn on each other. But we have chosen a different path. We don't sanction all the toys that have been somehow designed for killing or destroying human lives. Young people and children don't want toys of war. We boycott war films and cartoons. Then the film producers will think of making films on art, life and love, rather than tragic killings of this kind. Here, we only saw beauty and blessings." Thereafter, Frederick and then all of us sang our song for them:

*I write for you, oh Earth*
*You, our station and our refuge*
*For the world that blossoms in your womb,*
*you symbol of kindness*
*Remain for us*
*We are together, singular and unique*
*By the window that opens unto heaven*
*And in a night that tells us of a great secret*
*Remain for us*
*We are not afraid of the devils and their machine guns*
*We are not afraid of the tanks*
*that plow death and mines*
*that plant decadence and destruction*
*We shall make you flourish*
*Remain for us*
*We shall demolish the walls of separation and*
*build the bridges of love and kindness*

*Time will be ours*
*Remain for us*
*The stars are not that far from us*
*Look in our eyes*
*You will find a light full of hope*
*And we shall make you flourish again*
*And we shall invite the angels to the feast of love*
*Remain for us.*

Mr. Brosky had appeared on the screen. We all left our work to see what was new. Mr. Brosky was so happy that his complexion seemed red. He said: "Today, we along with Professor Ivanovich, Professor Kroshanka, Professor Nicola Patronovich,

Mr. Veronick, Mr. Volkof and Victor gathered here to thank you. Your message of love created a tumult on Earth. Children in groups from all regions, even from the farthest corners of the earth were looking for a center to join your cause. Well, they are right. Poor kids are right. They see that when it's time for them to work and live, they have no air to breathe, no proper food, no security in life. Even kids who have discovered these vital factors, have announced their alliance and unity. Naturally, we set up a center, hurriedly. Would you believe that millions have registered! Of course, this included adults. It's been years that scholars, futuristic people have been followers of a green environment, in short many people have written articles and given information, concerning the state of Earth. But no one truly understood. It was only your call of love and that from beyond the Earth and from the Mir Station that sounded good to the ears of the people of the world and made them alert. The children said that if five young people can be so unified and friendly so can we, only if these grown-ups let us."

We were exulted. We kept jumping up and down and hugging each other.

Mr. Brosky said: "This Mir Station has done a lot for us, but the most beautiful and the most important of those has been broadcasting your young voices full of life and your wishes. How

---

1 Zolgarnein: means the owner of a life of two centuries and also is the name of the king, who conquered the lands to the east and the west and God made him a prophet. *Farhang Asatiri* (The Encyclopedia of Mythology).

2 *Shahnameh* (The Book of Kings) is a book of poems by Ferdowsi, one of the great Iranian poets of 20th century. *Farhang Asatiri* (The Encyclopedia of Mythology, p. 206).

beautifully you sang this song and poem, kids. Soon we'll start a new phase in the life of the Earth. Now I ask you to sing your call of love one more time together, before the Soyuz arrives and brings you back to the Earth. Your voices are like the birds of the spring. Sing!

Printed by: Viba Press (P) Ltd., Okhla Phase-II, New Delhi-110020